A Manual of Worship

New Edition

Editors' Note: Boldface type within the text of worship materials indicates congregational response.

Purchase of this book grants the owner permission to reprint selected materials for one-time use in worship settings. Please use the following credit line: *A Manual of Worship, New Edition*, by John E. Skoglund and Nancy E. Hall; © 1993 by Judson Press. Used by permission.

A Manual of Worship

New Edition

John E. Skoglund
Nancy E. Hall

Judson Press ® Valley Forge

A Manual of Worship   New Edition

©1993
Judson Press, Valley Forge, PA 19482-0851

Library of Congress Cataloging-in-Publication Data
Skoglund, John E.
  A manual of worship / by John E. Skoglund and Nancy E. Hall. —
New Ed.
  p.   cm.
  ISBN 0-8170-1184-6
  1. Public worship—Handbooks, manuals, etc. 2. Free churches —
Liturgy—Texts. 3. Worship program. I. Hall, Nancy E. (Nancy
Elizabeth), 1951- II. Title.
BV25.S55 1993
264—dc20   92-46117
                                            CIP

Printed in the U.S.A.

Contents

90302

Preface

Since the earliest times when the followers of Jesus sat around a table to read together the Scriptures, to retell the stories of the one whom they called the Bread of Life, to pray, to sing, and to eat and drink in remembrance of him, worship has been the living heart of the Christian faith.

Yet all too often there have been times when worship has grown cold and formal, and the need has arisen for a time of renewal. The twentieth century has been such a time. Even before the century began, Benedictine monks of the Abbey of Solesmes had been at work on liturgical renewal. Centers for the renewal of worship sprang up in many places in Europe. Those who participated felt that their task was essentially pastoral. They sought to lead the people into a living experience of worship in which all participated. The Liturgical Movement, as it came to be called, reached its climax for the Church of Rome in Vatican II with the promulgation of the *Constitution on the Sacred Liturgy* on December 4, 1963.

Alongside the Roman Catholic movement Anglicans, Lutherans, and members of Reformed and free churches have sought ways to renew their worship. American Baptists in 1965 held a worship conference at Green Lake,

Wisconsin. Baptists participated in several ecumenical worship conferences, and books were published on worship themes. I was asked to prepare a service book, and the result was *A Manual of Worship*, published by Judson Press in 1968.

But the renewal movement has not stood still. Many changes have taken place. The formal Elizabethan language of worship has given way to contemporary expression. New versions of the Bible have brought new forms of the biblical text to the fore. The use of inclusive language has become a part of worship in many places. Thus from many quarters has come the call for a new book of worship designed for the free churches, and especially Baptists.

My colleague in worship and the arts at the American Baptist Seminary of the West, Nancy E. Hall, has joined me in the preparation of the manuscript. While the book is based upon the earlier manual, it is in reality a new work. The services have been completely updated, and much new worship material has been included. It is our hope that this volume will help to enrich the worship life of congregations and will serve as an aid to pastors, laypersons, and students of worship for years to come.

JOHN E. SKOGLUND

Acknowledgments

We wish to express our appreciation to those who have helped in various ways to bring this book into being. We thank Theodore Keaton, president of the American Baptist Seminary of the West, for communicating to Judson Press the need for a new book of worship and for the encouragement he gave to us in taking up the task. We are grateful to the congregation of the First Baptist Church of Berkeley, and our pastor, Esther Hargis, for their willingness to make trial use of some of the services and materials from this book in Sunday worship.

Many of the prayers included in this book originated with members of worship classes and seminars taught by John Skoglund at Colgate Rochester Divinity School during the late 1960s. While that material has been revised for this current edition, appreciation is still owed to those who were early contributors.

The Scripture quotations are, except in a very few instances, from the New Revised Standard Version of the Bible. In some cases, we have made minor changes in language to these Scripture quotations.

The authors acknowledge with thanks Augsburg Fortress Press, the consultation on Common Texts, and Oxford University Press for permission to reprint materials.

It has not always been possible to trace the source of some materials used in this book. If any have been included without suitable acknowledgment, such acts have been unintentional, and if we are notified of additional information, it will be included in future printings.

Finally, we are deeply grateful to our spouses, Daisy Skoglund and Mark Theodoropoulos. Their loving support in our lives goes far beyond the bounds of this project, and we dedicate this book to them.

JOHN E. SKOGLUND
NANCY E. HALL

Introduction

Free Church Worship

When the term *free church* is used in relation to worship, it means a church that does not have prescribed and required forms of worship. Some churches designated as free churches have liturgies that have been developed by the official body to which these congregations belong, but each remains free to use these worship forms, modify them, or ignore them. Included among the free churches are Adventists, Baptists, Congregationalists, Disciples of Christ, Mennonites, Methodists, Pentecostalists, Presbyterians and other Reformed groups, and many smaller Christian bodies.

Even though their worship is not bound by prescribed words and actions, the free churches claim that their worship embodies the same essential elements as the worship of the "liturgical" churches. Like all churches, their worship experience is to be found in the celebration of Word and Table and the human response present when "the Word is truly preached and the sacraments are rightly administered." For the free churches, as in all churches from apostolic times to the present, worship takes place primarily when a group of believers gather about the Lord's table to sing and pray, to hear the Scriptures read and preached, to break bread and drink wine in remembrance of Christ's death until he comes, and to offer praise and thanksgiving.

While the free churches have much in common with the worship in other churches, they have certain distinctive characteristics that set them apart.

1. *Simplicity.* When compared with Orthodox, Roman Catholic, or Episcopal worship, free church worship manifests an extreme simplicity, both in the way in which it is done and the setting in which it takes place.

The free church pioneers did away with the elaborate rituals and ceremonies of the established churches and replaced them with services of Bible reading, preaching, psalm singing, prayer, and rather infrequent observance of the Lord's Supper. They built unadorned chapels and meeting houses for their congregational gatherings. While in most free churches in recent times worship and place of meeting have been considerably enriched, there still remains a strong tenor of simplicity.

2. *Congregational Responsibility for Worship.* While a congregation may accept recommendations regarding worship from a denominational body, the congregation itself has primary responsibility for its worship life. The congregation designates a responsible body—such as deacons or elders—to develop worship policy. The execution of such policy will generally be left to the ministerial staff working with a lay worship committee or task force.

3. *Lay Participation in Worship.* While the pastor will generally lead the services, lay participation in Scripture readings, prayers, and litanies is common. In some free churches lay persons are licensed to preach and administer the sacraments. The whole congregation joins in the sing-

ing of hymns, in unison and responsive Scripture readings, amens, prayers, and litanies, and in some congregations, such as African American and Pentecostal, in simultaneous free prayer and dialogue with the pastor during the sermon.

4. *Extemporaneous Prayer*. While some free churches use written prayers, the general practice is free or extemporaneous prayer. In many free churches the only written or memorized prayer used in public worship is the Lord's Prayer. All other prayer is extemporaneous, and for the most part public prayers are created as they are spoken. Nevertheless, careful preparation is often made as to the topics to be covered and even the words to be used. Such is the case in the so-called pastoral prayer, which covers such elements of prayer as confession, petition, intercession, praise, and thanksgiving, and has had an important place in free church worship.

Laypersons are often called upon for prayer, and sometimes present the requests for prayer during the petitions and intercessions. The prayers included in a manual of worship such as this one can be used in public worship, but they can also help in developing and enriching extemporaneous prayer.

5. *Observance of the Christian Year*. In their beginning, the free churches for the most part rejected the observance of the festivals associated with the Christian year. These churches felt that the only Christian "holy day" was the first day of the week, the day of Christ's resurrection. Saints' days were eliminated, and even the observance of Christmas and Easter as religious holy days was frowned upon because of their pagan associations. Gradually, however, Christmas, Easter, and Pentecost have found places of observance in most free churches, and in many congre-

gations the periods of Advent, Epiphany, Lent, Pentecost, and Trinity or Kingdomtide are now followed.

Free churches do not require the use of lectionary readings, with sermons based upon these readings. Preachers are free to choose their own texts and topics. Yet, increasingly, free churches are not only following the seasons of the Christian year, but also using the Common Lectionary for Scripture readings and sermons. This manual has prayers and readings for the Christian year and provides in the appendix the Scripture texts for each Sunday of the year based upon the Common Lectionary.

6. *Sacraments*. The Lord's Supper and baptism are the sacraments of the free churches. (In some free churches, the word *ordinance*, rather than sacrament, is used.) The preaching of the Word is given high honor but not the status of a sacrament. Footwashing is practiced by some churches, notably the Church of the Brethren; this act is seen not as a sacrament but rather as part of the observance of the Lord's Supper. Matrimony, last rites, and the laying on of hands for the sick are important services of the church but are not considered sacraments. Except for the Disciples of Christ, most free churches observe the Lord's Supper quarterly, monthly, or, in the case of a few, once a year. Such infrequent observance does not mean that the free churches feel that the Supper is unimportant. Rather, the opposite is true.

When the free churches began, they looked upon the daily observances of the traditional churches as routine, legalistic, formal, and lacking in spiritual vitality. They felt that with less frequent celebration the Lord's Supper could be made more meaningful. They developed a service of preparation, and the Supper itself was a special service set apart from the regular worship of the congregation.

Furthermore, they felt that preaching had been long neglected, and they sought to bring it back into a place of primary importance. Thus, the worship service became a preaching service. In recent times some congregations are observing the Lord's Supper weekly, but such practices seek to correct an imbalance in worship which has long persisted in the free churches, not to minimize the importance of preaching. *The Service for the Lord's Day* presented in this manual includes both Word and Table, and even when the Supper is not observed Word and Table still provide the basic structure for public worship.

7. *Structure of Worship.* In Christian worship we respond from the depths of our being to God's mighty acts, particularly to the act of love, forgiveness, and reconciliation in Jesus Christ. Thus worship is a dialogue between God and God's people. God, who has been made known in Jesus Christ and whose acts are brought to remembrance in the reading of the Scriptures, in the preaching, and in the administration of the sacraments, comes to the faithful believer in worship as a living presence by the power of the Holy Spirit. The worshiper in turn responds to God's gracious self-giving by offering adoration, praise, thanksgiving, confession of sin, petition for God's presence, dedication of gifts and self to God's service, and prayer for others. It is this self-giving of God and the human response through prayer and action that provides the pattern of Christian worship.

These responsive elements of worship can readily be recognized as the various types of prayer. In the service of worship they need not be put together in one long pastoral prayer, but can become the responsive parts of the total worship service. The worship service then becomes common prayer and can be outlined as follows:

Preparation	Adoration
	Confession
The Word	Reading and Proclamation of God's Word
The Table	Petition
	Offertory (gifts, bread and wine, self)
	Dedication
	Remembrance and Thanksgiving
	Lord's Supper
	Intercession
Into the World	Dismissal and Blessing

This structure is the basis for *The Service for the Lord's Day* included in this manual. Hymns, sung psalms, gospel songs, choral anthems and responses, introits, doxologies, and glorias serve to enrich the service. Contemporary and traditional music brings the congregation into contact with the musical forms of the past, as well as the lively musical idiom of the present.

8. *Nontraditional Worship.* Freedom in worship has been a hallmark of the free church movement. It is little wonder that many free, as well as other, churches engage in liturgical experimentation in worship. Such services often feature popular rock and folk music, as well as multimedia presentations. The language and action used in nontraditional worship also have a strong appeal to many in the contemporary world. Because of their freedom from ecclesiastical control, the free churches are able to make a significant contribution to the revitalization of worship through creative experimentation.

In all worship, and particularly in nontraditional worship, the injunction of the Apostle must be kept in mind, that "all things should be done decently and in order." There are limits beyond which the enthusiast for worship renewal and revision cannot go without seriously damaging the basic reality of Christian worship.

9. *Inclusive and Formal Language.* In recent times there has been considerable debate over inclusive versus noninclusive and formal versus informal language in worship. Here again, as in so much of their life and thought, the free churches are free to choose. In this manual inclusive language is generally used. Text references have been included for the biblical material, and the worship leader is free to use any biblical translation. Similarly, less formal pronoun and verb forms have been employed in place of the Elizabethan language of the King James Version. Most biblical references are based on the New Revised Standard Version.

This manual is intended to help a congregation enrich and discipline itself in its worship life. In accord with the Reformed tradition, much of the material has been taken from the Scriptures. The orders, prayers, and other materials are offered as suggestions, but they are not intended to be binding upon any congregation as the only correct way to worship; rather, they can be a means to free a congregation for meaningful worship. This manual is presented in this spirit and for this use, that "the fellowship of the Holy Spirit," the local churches, might seek to develop truly congregational worship, using the gifts of all members, "so that together you may with one voice glorify God" (Romans 15:6).

Part 1

The Service
for the Lord's Day

Three orders of *The Service for the Lord's Day* are presented in this manual. The first includes the observance of the Lord's Supper. The second does not include the observance of the Supper, but nevertheless is governed by the Table without the bread and wine present. The third is a less formal service.

The services and materials included in the manual are intended simply as guides. They are developed in accordance with historic forms of worship, particularly those of the Reformed tradition, for the enrichment of the worship of the free churches.

In Part 2 you will find additional worship materials that may be used in these services.

The First and Second Services

Each service begins with an affirmation of purpose by the minister and congregation, followed by a processional, which in free church worship includes bringing in the Bible and placing it on the pulpit. This act affirms that the entire service is scripturally governed. Likewise, at the conclusion of the service the Bible is taken from the pulpit and placed on a stand by the door of the church. This recessional symbolizes the movement of the Word by means of the congregation into the world. When there is an observance of the Lord's Supper, a second processional takes place as the offerings of bread and wine and the gifts of the people are brought by the servers to the table. As the service concludes, the bread and wine, along with the Bible, are taken to a place by the door, to be taken symbolically by the people into the world.

Neither the first nor second service contains a pastoral prayer, but rather, numerous specific prayers: adoration, confession, petition, intercession, dedication, illumination, thanksgiving, and dismissal. These prayers are relatively short and provide the responses to the objective elements of the service, namely, Word and Table. The services are what has been rightly called "Common Prayer," that is, the prayers of the people of God.

Adoration follows the affirmation and processional. This part of the service may include words of adoration, an introit, a hymn, and a prayer of adoration/invocation. As in Isaiah 6, adoration leads to confession. The prophet beheld the glory of God filling the temple and, seeing his own sinfulness and that of the people, cried out, "Woe is me! I am lost, I am a man of unclean lips, and I live among a people of unclean lips; yet my eyes have seen the King, the Lord of hosts!" This portion of the service includes a call to confession, a prayer, the *Kyrie* or *Agnus Dei*, an affirmation of forgiveness, and some form of praise, such as the *Gloria Patri*, *Gloria in Excelsis*, or a hymn.

Confession and praise for sin forgiven lead to the sharing of the peace, followed by the Ministry of the Word, the central part of the first section of the service. This section includes Scripture lessons, a prayer before the sermon, the sermon, and an affirmation of faith.

The second section of the first service includes the Lord's Supper. The second service does not include the Supper as a visible observance; nevertheless, the pattern of the service follows essentially the same lines as the first and includes those prayers associated with the Supper.

The offertory is the transition between the first and second sections of both services. In the full service, the offertory consists of the gifts of the people, the bread and the wine of the Supper, and the dedication of the members of the congregation. Included in the offertory are a call, the processional, and prayers of petition and dedication. If a hymn of invitation is desired it can be most properly included as a part of the offertory, for it is at this point in the service that commitment to Christian discipleship in response to the message of the Word can most appropriately take place.

The Ministry of the Table includes an invitation to communion and a response, an affirmation of unity and peace, the words of institution, prayers of remembrance and thanksgiving, a prayer for the presence of the Holy Spirit, the Lord's Prayer, the breaking and distribution of the bread and the pouring and distribution of the wine, communion, and the *Sanctus*. A hymn may be sung.

The prayers included in the Ministry of the Table are of vital importance. The prayers of remembrance (*anamnesis*) and thanksgiving (*eucharistia*) express the joy for God's great gift in Jesus Christ. In the ancient church, as well as in some present-day churches, the service is called the Eucharist, after the prayer of thanksgiving. The prayer for the presence of the Holy Spirit, or the *epiclesis*, is a petition not only for the presence of the Spirit, but also that

Christ may become a living reality in the lives of the worshipers through the symbolic act of eating the bread and drinking of the cup.

The service concludes with a prayer of dismissal and blessing. This prayer stresses the true role of the church, which is to give witness of God's love for the world and to minister to those who have special needs.

The second service is structured like the first, except that it does not include the visible observance of the Lord's Supper. Yet even in this service the Supper governs the second half: although the elements are not present, they are symbolized in the offertory and the acts of remembrance and thanksgiving.

Parent-child dedication, baptism, the licensing, ordination, or installation of a minister, the installation of church officers, marriage, and other special observances can take place within *The Service for the Lord's Day* at the time of the offertory, for in each of these ceremonies those involved are offering themselves to God, asking for God's blessing in their new relationship and service.

Music can enrich the service of worship at many points. But music should serve as an aid to worship and be suitable to the various parts of the service in which it is included. Preludes, postludes, anthems, and responses, as well as introits, glorias, doxologies, hymns, and psalms, all have their appropriate places. When done skillfully they can greatly enhance worship and give glory to God.

The primary function of the choir is to strengthen congregational participation in worship, as both teacher and leader. When choral or solo music is used, it should be movable. If, for example, its theme is adoration, it should come at the beginning of the service; if penitential, at the time of the prayer of confession. A sung psalm from the Old Testament can be included at the time of the Scripture readings. Music can be appropriately done at other parts of the service, but if music is done solely for performance it has no place in worship.

Hymns play a major role in worship. As with other musical selections, hymns should come at the parts of the service where their themes are germane. Many hymns are prayers and ought to be sung in a spirit of devotion. Through hymns the congregation can adore, confess, intercede, petition, dedicate, and give thanks. Congregational singing offers the possibility of introducing variety in worship. This was clearly evident even in the early church, as the apostle Paul wrote to the Christians in Colossae, "With gratitude in your hearts sing psalms, hymns, and spiritual songs to God" (Colossians 3:16).

The Third Service

The third, less formal service is called *A Service of Praise and Prayer*. It is structured according to the parts of prayer: adoration, confession, intercession, petition, dedication, remembrance, thanksgiving, and dismissal. It can be done with or without the Lord's Supper. It offers considerable latitude as to material to be included, and thus gives to the minister and worship leader freedom to modify it according to special situations.

Outline of the Service for the Lord's Day (with the Lord's Supper)

AFFIRMATION OF PURPOSE AND ENTRY OF SCRIPTURES

ADORATION
  Words of adoration, invitation, or promise
  Hymn

Prayer of adoration or invocation

CONFESSION
Call
Prayer of confession
Kyrie or *Agnus Dei*
Assurance of forgiveness
Praise: *Gloria Patri, Gloria in Excelsis*, or a hymn

THE PEACE

MINISTRY OF THE WORD
Scripture lessons
Prayer before the sermon
Sermon
Hymn of invitation
Affirmation of faith

MINISTRY OF THE TABLE
Prayers of the people (petitions and intercessions)
Offertory: gifts, bread and wine, and self
Doxology or hymn
Prayer of dedication
Invitation to communion and response
Affirmation of unity
Institution of the Lord's Supper
Prayers of remembrance and thanksgiving
Prayer for the presence of the Holy Spirit
The Lord's (or Disciples') Prayer
Breaking and distribution of the bread
Eating of the bread
Pouring and distribution of the wine
Drinking of the wine
Agnus Dei and prayer of commitment

The Service for the Lord's Day

   Hymn and recessional of Scriptures and bread and wine
   Dismissal: ascription of glory, benedictions, and
   blessings

The Service for the Lord's Day (with the Lord's Supper)

Affirmation of Purpose and Entry of Scriptures

On a stand near the door of the church shall be placed the Bible, the bread and wine for the Lord's Supper, and a receptacle where the people may place their gifts as they enter.

At the appointed hour, the people stand (those who prefer may remain seated) and the minister or lay worship leader says the following or other suitable words:

Why are we gathered in this place at this hour?
   We are gathered as the people of God to offer praise and thanksgiving to God, to confess our sin, to pray for the world, and to rededicate ourselves as God's servants.

Then let us join together in the worship of God, to whom belongs blessing and glory and wisdom and thanksgiving and honor and power and might forever and ever.

                                                     Revelation 7:12

The people are seated, and a prelude is played as a lay leader brings the Bible to the table, lectern, or pulpit.

Adoration

The minister or lay leader says one of the following or other suitable words of adoration, invitation, or promise (or the choir may sing an introit):

Our help is in the name of God, who made heaven and earth.   Psalm 124:8

Come, let us sing to God; let us make a joyful noise to the rock of our salvation! Let us come into God's presence with thanksgiving; let us make a joyful noise with songs of praise!   Psalm 95:1-2

Then shall a hymn of adoration be sung, followed by a prayer of adoration:

Great are you, O God, and greatly to be praised. Great is your love as shown in Christ Jesus. We would praise you without ceasing, for you have made us for yourself, and our hearts find no rest until they rest in you. Amen.

Confession

The minister says:
If we say that we that we have no sin, we deceive ourselves, and the truth is not in us. If we confess our sins, God, who is faithful and just, will forgive us our sins and cleanse us from all unrighteousness.   1 John 1:8-9

Let us therefore humbly confess our sin to God and seek forgiveness through Jesus Christ our Savior.

Then shall be offered a prayer of confession:

Almighty and most merciful God, we have erred and strayed from your ways like lost sheep. We have followed too much the desires of our hearts. We have offended against your holy laws. We have left undone those things which we ought to have done; and we have done those things which we ought not to have done; and there is no health in us. Have mercy on us. Spare those who confess their faults. Restore those who are penitent, according to your promises declared in Jesus Christ. And grant, O most merciful God, for his sake, that we may hereafter live a godly, righteous, and sober life, to the glory of your holy name. Amen.

or

Have mercy on us, O God, according to your steadfast love; according to your abundant mercy blot out our transgressions. Wash us thoroughly from our iniquities, and cleanse us from our sins. Create in us clean hearts, O God, and put a new and right spirit within us. Do not cast us away from your presence, and do not take your Holy Spirit from us. Restore to us the joy of your salvation, and sustain in us a willing spirit. Amen.   Psalm 51:1-2,10-12

After the prayer of confession there shall be silence in which there is personal confession of sin; then the Kyrie *may be said or sung:*

Lord, have mercy upon us.
Christ, have mercy upon us.

Lord, have mercy upon us.

Then the minister offers words of assurance:
The saying is sure and worthy of full acceptance, that Christ Jesus came into the world to save sinners. So if anyone is in Christ, there is a new creation: everything old has passed away; see, everything has become new! To the Ruler of the ages, immortal, invisible, the only God, be honor and glory forever and ever. Amen.   1 Timothy 1:15,17
2 Corinthians 5:17

or

God's love for us is proved in that while we still were sinners Christ died for us. There is therefore now no condemnation for those who are in Christ Jesus.   Romans 5:8;8:1

The Gloria Patri, *the* Gloria in Excelsis, *or a hymn of praise is now sung.*

The Peace

The minister now says:
The peace of Christ be with you.
And also with you.

The congregation and worship leaders greet one another with a handshake or embrace and repeat the words of peace.

Ministry of the Word

The minister or worship leader opens the Bible to the first lesson and says:
God offers to us in the Scriptures words of life which through faith can become for us the Word of life.
The first reading is from _____ .

An Old Testament and/or an Epistle lesson may be read, followed by the responsive reading of a psalm or the singing of a hymn or psalm.

After each lesson the reader says:
Here ends the first (second, or third) reading.

After each reading the people may say:
Praise be to you, O God.

The reader opens the Bible to the Gospel lesson and says:
The Gospel reading is from _____ .

After the reading of the Gospel the people may say:
Praise be to you, O Christ.

The lessons having been read, the minister says:
Let us pray.
Gracious God, by your Holy Spirit cause the words that have been read to become for us the very Word of life.
Amen.

or

May the words of my mouth,
And the meditations of our hearts be acceptable to you, our rock and our redeemer. Amen.

A sermon based upon one or more of the Scriptures read shall be preached.

After the sermon an invitation may be given to any who feel called to confess their faith in Christ or renew their obedience to him publicly. A hymn of invitation may be sung.

The people may then stand and together affirm their faith, using the Apostles' Creed, a scriptural affirmation of faith, or an affirmation of faith or a covenant of the congregation.

Ministry of the Table

The minister or worship leader, following an ancient custom of the church, calls for the members of the congregation to express their joys and concerns. After each bidding a short prayer of petition or intercession may be offered, or after all the biddings have been given, the minister or worship leader may offer a prayer on behalf of the people.

The minister or lay leader shall say an offertory sentence. The gifts and the bread and wine are then brought by the servers to the table as the Doxology or a hymn is sung. The servers take their places about the table for the serving of the Lord's Supper. After receiving the gifts, the minister or lay leader shall offer the following or another offertory prayer:

We offer to you, O God, this bread and wine, to be set apart for the remembrance of the passion of Jesus Christ, our Lord and Savior. We present to you these gifts, thanking you for the strength and skill to do our daily work. Together with them we offer ourselves, asking you to strengthen us, that all our work may be your service, all our meals a thankful remembrance of your bounty to us. May we be a living sacrifice, holy and acceptable to you; through Jesus Christ our Lord. **Amen.**

The minister, standing at the table, shall say:
The Gospel tells us that as the risen Christ sat at table with two of his followers he was made known to them in the breaking of bread. At this table we invite all who believe in him and who are in fellowship with one another to partake of this, the Supper of the Lord. Let us pray together:

Our God, we who are at this table trust that through the eating of the bread and drinking of the cup we shall come to a thankful remembrance of Jesus Christ, and that, by your Holy Spirit, Christ will come to dwell within and among us. Amen.

The minister, taking the bread and the cup, says:
Hear the words of the Institution of the Lord's Supper as written by Paul the apostle: The Lord Jesus on the night when he was betrayed took a loaf of bread, and when he had given thanks, he broke it and said, ''This is my body that is for you. Do this in remembrance of me.'' In the same way he took the cup also, after supper, saying, ''This cup is the new covenant in my blood. Do this, as often as you drink it, in remembrance of me.'' For as often as you eat this bread and drink the cup, you proclaim the Lord's death until he comes. 1 Corinthians 11:23-26

This is the joyful feast of the people of God. People will come from east and west, from north and south, and will eat in the kingdom of God. Luke 13:29

The minister or a lay leader says:
Let us give thanks to God.
Gracious God, in whom we live and move and have our being, we lift our hearts and offer thanks to you for the wonders of the world about us, for humankind and the richness of love, for each new day of forgiveness and grace. With thanksgiving we remember the one who was with you from the beginning, through whom all things were made, whose life is the light of the world and who became flesh and lived among us as Jesus the Christ. For his life and ministry, for his teaching and example, and for his love,

We thank you, O God.
For his victory on the cross,
We thank you, O God.
For the hope that comes through his resurrection,
We thank you, O God.
For the promise that in him all things shall be made new,
We thank you, O God.
Grant, O God, that your Holy Spirit may be with us, and that through the bread and wine set apart for remembrance and thanksgiving Christ may come to dwell among us, and through him we may know you, whom to know is life eternal. **Amen.**

Let us in silence offer our prayer for Christ's presence within and among us.

A time of silence is observed. The minister then says:
Let us pray as Christ taught his disciples:
Our Father in heaven, hallowed be your name. Your kingdom come. Your will be done, on earth as it is in heaven. Give us this day our daily bread. And forgive us our debts, as we also have forgiven our debtors. And do not bring us to the time of trial, but rescue us from the evil one. For the kingdom and the power and the glory are yours forever. Amen.

The minister shall break the bread and give it to the servers, who in turn shall give it to the people. After all have been served, the minister shall say:
Jesus said, "This is my body, which is given for you. Do this in remembrance of me."   Luke 22:19

The minister then gives the wine to the servers, who in turn give it to the people. After all have been served, the minister says:

Jesus said, "Drink from it, all of you; for this is my blood of the covenant, which is poured out for many for the forgiveness of sins." Matthew 26:28

After a time of silence, the minister may use the words of the Agnus Dei *followed by a prayer of commitment:*
Behold, the Lamb of God, who takes away the sin of the world!
Lamb of God, who takes away the sin of the world, have mercy on us.
Lamb of God, who takes away the sin of the world, grant us your peace.
Most merciful God, take our hands, which have held that which is consecrated, and work through them;
Take our lips, which have tasted the signs of the body and blood of our Lord, and speak through them;
Take our bodies, which have received the bread and wine, and make them fit temples of your Spirit;
Take our minds and mold them, that our thoughts may be your thoughts;
Take our hearts and fill them with your love, that we may truly serve you in the world. Amen.

Into the World

As a hymn is sung, the servers may take the Bible and the remaining bread and wine from the table to the place by the entry.

Then shall the minister say one of the following or some other suitable words of dismissal:
Go forth into the world in peace. Be of good courage; hold fast to that which is good; render to no one evil for evil.

Strengthen the fainthearted, support the weak, help the afflicted, honor all persons. Love and serve God, rejoicing in the power of the Holy Spirit. The grace of the Lord Jesus Christ, the love of God, and the fellowship of the Holy Spirit be with you all. **Amen.**

or

God bless you and keep you. God's face shine upon you and be gracious to you. God look upon you with love and give you peace. **Amen.** Numbers 6:24-26

Outline of the Service for the Lord's Day (without the Lord's Supper)

AFFIRMATION OF PURPOSE AND ENTRY OF THE SCRIPTURES

ADORATION
  Words of adoration, invitation, or promise
  Hymn
  Prayer of adoration or invocation

CONFESSION
  Call
  Prayer of confession
  Kyrie
  Assurance of forgiveness
  Praise: *Gloria Patri, Gloria in Excelsis,* or a hymn

THE PEACE

MINISTRY OF THE WORD
  Scripture lessons
  Prayer before the sermon
  Sermon
  Hymn of invitation
  Affirmation of faith

MINISTRY OF THE TABLE
    Prayers of the people (petitions and intercessions)
    Offering of gifts and self
    Doxology or hymn
    Prayers of dedication and thanksgiving
    The Lord's (Disciples') Prayer

INTO THE WORLD
    Hymn and recessional of Scriptures
    Dismissal: ascription of glory, benedictions, and
        blessings

The Service for the Lord's Day (without the Lord's Supper)

Affirmation of Purpose and Entry of Scriptures

On a stand near the door of the church shall be placed the Bible and a receptacle where the people may place their gifts as they enter.

At the appointed hour, the people stand (those who prefer may remain seated) and the minister or lay worship leader says the following or other suitable words:
Why are we gathered in this place at this hour?
We are gathered as the people of God to offer praise and thanksgiving to God, to confess our sin, to pray for the world, and to rededicate ourselves as God's servants.

Then let us join together in the worship of God, to whom belongs blessing and glory and wisdom and thanksgiving and honor and power and might forever and ever.
                                                    Revelation 7:12

The people are seated, and a prelude is played as a lay leader brings the Bible to the pulpit.

Adoration

The minister or lay leader says one of the following or another suitable word of adoration, invitation, or promise (or the choir may sing an introit):

Our help is in the name of God, who made heaven and earth.   Psalm 124:8

Come, let us sing to God; let us make a joyful noise to the rock of our salvation! Let us come into God's presence with thanksgiving; let us make a joyful noise with songs of praise!   Psalm 95:1-2

Then shall a hymn of adoration be sung, followed by a prayer of adoration:

Great are you, O God, and greatly to be praised. Great is your love as shown in Christ Jesus. We would praise you without ceasing, for you have made us for yourself, and our hearts find no rest until they rest in you. Amen.

Confession

The minister says:

If we say that we that we have no sin, we deceive ourselves, and the truth is not in us. If we confess our sins, God, who is faithful and just, will forgive us our sins and cleanse us from all unrighteousness.   1 John 1:8-9

Let us therefore humbly confess our sin to God and seek forgiveness through Jesus Christ our Savior.

Then shall be offered a prayer of confession:

Almighty and most merciful God, we have erred and strayed from your ways like lost sheep. We have followed too much the desires of our hearts. We have offended against your holy laws. We have left undone those things which we ought to have done; and we have done those things which we ought not to have done; and there is no health in us. Have mercy on us. Spare those who confess their faults. Restore those who are penitent, according to your promises declared in Jesus Christ. And grant, O most merciful God, for his sake, that we may hereafter live a godly, righteous, and sober life, to the glory of your holy name. Amen.

or

Have mercy on us, O God, according to your steadfast love; according to your abundant mercy blot out our transgressions. Wash us thoroughly from our iniquities, and cleanse us from our sin. Create in us clean hearts, O God, and put a new and right spirit within us. Do not cast us away from your presence, and do not take your holy spirit from us. Restore to us the joy of your salvation, and sustain in us a willing spirit. Amen. Psalm 51:1-2,10-12

After the prayer of confession there shall be silence in which there is personal confession of sin; then the Kyrie *may be said or sung:*

Lord, have mercy upon us.

Christ, have mercy upon us.

Lord, have mercy upon us.

Then the minister offers words of assurance:

The saying is sure and worthy of full acceptance, that Christ

Jesus came into the world to save sinners. So if anyone is in Christ, there is a new creation: everything old has passed away; see, everything has become new! To the Ruler of the ages, immortal, invisible, the only God, be honor and glory forever and ever. Amen.   1 Timothy 1:15,17
                                                    2 Corinthians 5:17

or

God's love for us is proved in that while we were still sinners Christ died for us. There is therefore now no condemnation for those who are in Christ Jesus.   Romans 5:8;8:1

The Gloria Patri, *the* Gloria in Excelsis, *or a hymn of praise is now sung.*

The Peace

The minister now says:
The peace of Christ be with you.
And also with you.

The congregation and worship leaders greet one another with a handshake or embrace and repeat the words of peace.

Ministry of the Word

The minister or worship leader opens the Bible to the first lesson and says:
God offers to us in the Scriptures words of life which through faith can become for us the Word of life.
The first reading is from _____ .

An Old Testament and/or an Epistle lesson may be read, followed by the responsive reading of a psalm or the singing of a hymn or psalm.

After each lesson the reader says:
Here ends the first (second, third) reading.

After each reading the people may say:
    Praise be to you, O God.

The reader opens the Bible to the Gospel lesson and says:
The Gospel reading is from _____ .

After the reading of the Gospel the people may say:
    Praise be to you, O Christ.

The lessons having been read, the minister says:
Let us pray.
Gracious God, by your Holy Spirit cause the words that have been read to become for us the very Word of life. **Amen.**

or

May the words of my mouth,
    And the meditations of our hearts be acceptable to you, our rock and our redeemer. Amen.

A sermon based upon one or more of the Scriptures read shall be preached.

After the sermon an invitation may be given to any who feel called to confess their faith in Christ or renew their commitment to Christ. A hymn of invitation may be sung.

The people may then stand and together affirm their faith, using the Apostles' Creed, a scriptural affirmation of faith, or an affirmation of faith or a covenant of the congregation.

Ministry of the Table

After the people are seated the minister says:
Our Lord called us to be a royal priesthood that we might

offer prayers for ourselves and for all peoples.
Let us pray.

The minister or worship leader, following an ancient custom of the church, calls for the members of the congregation to express their joys and concerns. After each bidding, a short prayer of petition or intercession may be offered, or after all the biddings have been given, the minister or worship leader may offer a prayer on behalf of the people.

The minister or lay leader shall say an offertory sentence. The gifts are then brought to the table as the Doxology or a hymn is sung. After receiving the gifts the minister or lay leader shall offer the following or another offertory prayer:

We present to you, O God, these gifts, thanking you for the strength and skill to do our daily work. Together with them we offer ourselves, asking you to strengthen us, that all our work may be your service, all our meals a thankful remembrance of your bounty to us, and that we might be a living sacrifice, holy and acceptable to you; through Jesus Christ our Lord. **Amen.**

Let us give thanks to God.
Gracious God, in whom we live and move and have our being, we lift our hearts and offer thanks to you for the wonders of the world about us, for humankind and the richness of love, for each new day of forgiveness and grace. With thanksgiving we remember the one who was with you from the beginning, through whom all things were made, whose life is the light of the world and who became flesh and lived among us as Jesus the Christ. For his life and ministry, for his teaching and example, and for his love,
   We thank you, O God.

For his victory on the cross,
We thank you, O God.
For the hope that comes through his resurrection,
We thank you, O God.
For the promise that in him all things shall be made new,
We thank you, O God.
Grant, O God, that your Holy Spirit may be with us, and that Christ may come to dwell among us, and through him we may know you, whom to know is life eternal. **Amen.**

Let us in silence offer our prayer for Christ's presence within and among us.

A time of silence is observed. The minister then says:
Let us pray as Christ taught us.
Our Father in heaven, hallowed be your name. Your kingdom come. Your will be done, on earth as it is in heaven. Give us this day our daily bread. And forgive us our debts, as we also have forgiven our debtors. And do not bring us to the time of trial, but rescue us from the evil one. For the kingdom and the power and the glory are yours forever. Amen.

Into the World

As a hymn is sung the servers may take the Bible to the place by the entry.

Then shall the minister say one of the following or some other suitable words of dismissal:
Go forth into the world in peace. Be of good courage; hold fast to that which is good; render to no one evil for evil. Strengthen the fainthearted, support the weak, help the

afflicted, honor all persons. Love and serve God, rejoicing in the power of the Holy Spirit. The grace of the Lord Jesus Christ, the love of God, and the fellowship of the Holy Spirit be with you all. **Amen.**

or

God bless you and keep you. God's face shine upon you and be gracious to you. God look upon you with love and give you peace. **Amen.**   Numbers 6:24-26

Outline of a Service of Praise and Prayer (with the Lord's Supper)

ADORATION
    Call to worship
    Hymn of praise
    Prayer

CONFESSION
    Call to confession
    Silent confession
    Assurance of forgiveness
    Sung response

THE PEACE

MINISTRY OF THE WORD
    Scripture lessons
    Sermon or meditation

PETITION AND INTERCESSION
    Prayers of the people

MINISTRY OF THE TABLE
    Call to offering
    Gathering of gifts

Doxology or hymn
Prayer of dedication
Invitation to communion
Words of institution
Prayer of remembrance and thanksgiving
Sharing of the bread and cup

DISMISSAL AND BLESSING
Hymn for going out
Benediction

A Service of Praise and Prayer
(with the Lord's Supper)

Adoration

Call to Worship
The people stand; those who prefer may remain seated.
Lord, we come before you this day as part of the human
family.
Inspire us, O God; open our hearts.
We come in our diversity to catch your vision of unity.
Inspire us, O God; open our eyes.
We come to hear your challenging word of truth.
Inspire us, O God; open our ears.
We come to thank you for your gifts of beauty, joy, and
hope.
**O God of love, vision, and truth, we praise your
blessed name.**

Hymn of Praise

Prayer
Eternal God, we gather in your presence and reach out

to you in prayer. We thank you for your constant love and boundless wisdom. We praise you for the glory of creation and the joy of our faith. So be with us now in this hour of worship, for it is in answer to your call that we gather. **Amen.**

Confession

Call to Confession

God was in Christ, and in Christ the world was reconciled to God. Therefore we come, in the Reconciler's name, to claim healing within and among us. The One who received sinners and ate with them invites us to share in the feast of God's forgiving love. Let us confess our sin.

Silent Confession

Assurance of Forgiveness

Joyfully, God offers us forgiveness for our sins and opens the path to new life in Christ. Let us celebrate this abundant grace.
   Thanks be to God!

Sung Response

The final verse of the Hymn of Praise or the first verse of "Amazing Grace" may be sung, or another appropriate response.

The Peace

Passing of the Peace

May the peace of Christ be with you always.
   And also with you.

The people exchange greetings of peace with a handshake or embrace, and then are seated.

Ministry of the Word

Scripture Lessons

Sermon or Meditation

Petition and Intercession

Prayers of the People
The minister or worship leader may ask for congregational expressions of joy and concern, followed by prayers of petition and intercession.

Ministry of the Table

Call to Offering
Our worship is complete when we bring all of our resources to receive God's blessing and fulfill God's purposes. In joyous gratitude we bring more than money; we bring bread, cup, and ourselves as an offering to God.

Gathering of Gifts

Doxology or Hymn
The people stand and sing a Doxology or hymn of commitment as the gifts, bread, and cup are brought forward.

**Praise God, from whom all blessings flow;
Praise God, all creatures here below;
Praise God with all the heavenly host;
Creator, Christ, and Holy Ghost. Amen.**

Prayer of Dedication

For all the riches you bestow, for all the good you supply, for all the guidance you offer day by day,

We give thanks, gracious God.

All that we give we owe to you, and life itself is a gift from your hand.

We dedicate our offerings, this bread and cup, and our lives to your honor and glory. Amen.

The people are seated.

Invitation to Communion

Words of Institution

Our Lord Jesus on the night he was betrayed took a loaf of bread, gave thanks to God, broke it, and said, "This is my body that is for you. Do this in memory of me." In the same way, after the supper he took the cup and said, "This cup is God's new covenant, sealed with my blood. Whenever you drink it, do so in memory of me." This means that every time we eat this bread and drink from this cup we proclaim the Lord's death until he comes. 1 Corinthians 11:23-26, adapted

Prayer of Remembrance and Thanksgiving

In remembrance of all that Christ has done for us, we offer praise and thanksgiving, proclaiming the good news of our faith:

Christ has died; Christ is risen; Christ will come again.

By your Spirit, Lord, make us one with Christ, one with each other, and one in ministry to all the world. **Amen.**

Sharing of the Bread and Cup

Dismissal and Blessing

Hymn for Going Out
The people stand.

Benediction
May the peace and glory of God which is beyond all understanding keep our hearts and minds in the knowledge and love of God and in Jesus Christ, our Savior. **Amen.**

Outline of a Service of Praise and Prayer (without the Lord's Supper)

ADORATION
Call to worship
Hymn of praise
Prayer

CONFESSION
Call to confession
Silent confession
Assurance of forgiveness
Sung response

THE PEACE

MINISTRY OF THE WORD
Scripture lessons
Sermon or meditation

PETITION AND INTERCESSION
Prayers of the people

DEDICATION AND THANKSGIVING
    Call to offering
    Gathering of gifts
    Doxology or hymn
    Prayer of dedication

DISMISSAL AND BLESSING
    Hymn for going out
    Benediction

A Service of Praise and Prayer (without the Lord's Supper)

Adoration

Call to Worship
The people stand; those who prefer may remain seated.
Lord, we come before you this day as part of the human family.
Inspire us, O God; open our hearts.
We come in our diversity to catch your vision of unity.
Inspire us, O God; open our eyes.
We come to hear your challenging word of truth.
Inspire us, O God; open our ears.
We come to thank you for your gifts of beauty, joy, and hope.
O God of love, vision, and truth, we praise your blessed name.

Hymn of Praise

Prayer

Eternal God, we gather in your presence and reach out to you in prayer. We thank you for your constant love and boundless wisdom. We praise you for the glory of creation and the joy of our faith. So be with us now in this hour of worship, for it is in answer to your call that we gather. **Amen.**

Confession

Call to Confession

God was in Christ, and in Christ the world was reconciled to God. Therefore we come, in the Reconciler's name, to claim healing within and among us. The One who received sinners and ate with them invites us to share in the feast of God's forgiving love. Let us confess our sin.

Silent Confession

Assurance of Forgiveness

Joyfully, God offers us forgiveness for our sins and opens the path to new life in Christ. Let us celebrate this abundant grace.
   Thanks be to God!

Sung Response

The final verse of the Hymn of Praise or the first verse of "Amazing Grace" may be sung, or another appropriate response.

The Peace

Passing of the Peace

May the peace of Christ be with you always.
   And also with you.

The people exchange greetings of peace with a hand-shake or embrace, and then are seated.

Ministry of the Word

Scripture Lessons

Sermon or Meditation

Petition and Intercession

Prayers of the People
The minister or worship leader may ask for congregational expressions of joy and concern, followed by prayers of petition and intercession.

Dedication and Thanksgiving

Call to Offering
Our worship is complete when we bring all of our resources to receive God's blessing and fulfill God's purposes. In joyous gratitude we bring more than money; we bring ourselves as an offering to God.

Gathering of Gifts

Doxology or Hymn
The people shall stand and sing a Doxology or hymn of commitment as the gifts are brought forward.
Praise God, from whom all blessings flow;
Praise God, all creatures here below;
Praise God with all the heavenly host;
Creator, Christ, and Holy Ghost. Amen.

Prayer of Dedication

> For all the riches you bestow, for all the good you supply, for all the guidance you offer day by day,
>
> **We give thanks, gracious God.**
>
> All that we give we owe to you, and life itself is a gift from your hand.
>
> **We dedicate our lives with our offerings to your honor and glory. Amen.**

Dismissal and Blessing

Hymn for Going Out

Benediction

> May the peace and glory of God which is beyond all understanding keep our hearts and minds in the knowledge and love of God and in Jesus Christ, our Savior. **Amen.**

Part 2

Materials for Public Worship

The materials for public worship follow the order of *The Service for the Lord's Day*. As in the service, the language of these materials seeks to be inclusive, in so far as possible. While most of the biblical material is based on the New Revised Standard Version of the Bible, where necessary these texts have been modified in the interest of inclusiveness. Text references have been included to enable the worship leader to consult and use other versions of the Bible.

Adoration

Words of Adoration

Surely God is in this place. This is none other than the house of God.   Genesis 28:16-17

Give thanks and call upon God's name, make known God's deeds among the peoples. Sing praises, tell of all God's wonderful works.   1 Chronicles 16:8-9

Blessed are you, O God, forever and ever. Yours, O God, are the greatness, the power, the glory, the victory, and the majesty; for all that is in the heavens and on the earth is yours; you are exalted as head above all.

1 Chronicles 29:10-11

It is good to give thanks to God, to sing praises to your name, O Most High; to declare your steadfast love in the morning, and your faithfulness by night.   Psalm 92:1-2

Come, let us sing to God; let us make a joyful noise to the rock of our salvation! Let us come into God's presence with thanksgiving; let us make a joyful noise with songs of praise.   Psalm 95:1-2

Come, let us worship and bow down, let us kneel before the Lord, our Maker! For the Lord is our God, and we are the people of God's pasture, and the flock that is led by God's hand.   Psalm 95:6-7

O sing to God a new song; sing to God, all the earth. Sing and bless God's name; tell of salvation from day to day. Declare God's glory among the nations, and the marvelous works of God among all the peoples. For great is God and greatly to be praised.   Psalm 96:1-4

Give thanks to God, for God is good; God's steadfast love endures forever, and God's faithfulness to all generations.

Psalm 100:4-5

Give thanks to God; make known God's deeds among the peoples. Sing, sing praises to God; tell of all God's wonderful works. Let the hearts of those who seek their Creator rejoice.   Psalm 105:1-3

Praise God! Blessed be the name of God from this time on and forevermore. From the rising of the sun to its setting the name of God is to be praised.　　　Psalm 113:1-3

This is the day that God has made; let us rejoice and be glad in it. Blessed is the one who comes in the name of the Lord.　　　Psalm 118:24,26

Our help is in the name of God, who made heaven and earth.　　　Psalm 124:8

Praise God! How good it is to sing praises to our God; for God is gracious, and a song of praise is fitting.

Psalm 147:1

Praise God! Praise God in the sanctuary; praise God in the mighty firmament! Praise God for mighty deeds; praise God's surpassing greatness! Let everything that breathes praise God! Praise God!　　　Psalm 150:1-2,6

Give thanks! Call on God's name; make known God's deeds among the nations. Sing praises to God, for God has done gloriously; let this be known in all the earth. Shout aloud and sing for joy, for great in your midst is the Holy One.　　　Isaiah 12:4-6

You are worthy, our God, to receive glory and honor and power, for you created all things, and by your will they existed and were created.　　　Revelation 4:11

Amen! Blessing and glory and wisdom and thanksgiving and honor and power and might be to our God forever and ever! Amen.　　　Revelation 7:12

Glory to God the Creator and to Christ and to the Holy Spirit: as it was in the beginning, is now and shall be forever and ever. Amen. *Gloria Patri*, adapted

Blessed are you, O God, who has given to humankind the insight and knowledge to understand your wonders, to discern your truth, to tell forth your abundant mercies. Blessed are you, O God. Dead Sea Scrolls

We praise you, O God; we acknowledge you to be the ruler over all. All the earth worships you, God everlasting.
Te Deum

Holy, holy, holy, Lord God of hosts, heaven and earth are full of your glory: Glory be to you, O God most high. Amen. *Sanctus*

Magnify the Lord with me, and let us exalt the Lord's name together.
Hallelujah! For the Lord our God the Almighty reigns. Let us rejoice and exult and give God the glory. Psalm 34:3; Revelation 19:6-7

Come let us sing to God; let us make a joyful noise to the rock of our salvation!
Let us come into God's presence with thanksgiving; let us make a joyful noise with songs of praise.
Psalm 95:1-2

Sing to God a new song; sing to God, all the earth.
Sing to God, bless God's name; tell of salvation from day to day.

Declare God's glory among the nations, and God's marvelous works among all the peoples.

For great is God, and greatly to be praised.

Psalm 96:1-4

Enter God's gates with thanksgiving, and God's courts with praise. Give thanks; bless God's name.

For God is good; God's steadfast love endures forever, and God's faithfulness to all generations.

Psalm 100:4-5

Praise God, all you nations! Extol God, all you peoples!

For great is God's steadfast love toward us, and God's faithfulness endures forever. Praise God!

Psalm 117

This is the day that God has made;

Let us rejoice and be glad in it.   Psalm 118:24

You are worthy, our God, to receive glory and honor and power, for you created all things, and by your will they existed and were created.

Holy, holy, holy, the Lord God the Almighty, who was and is and is to come, you are worthy to receive glory and honor and power.   Revelation 4:8,11

Praise our God, all you who are God's servants.

Hallelujah! For the Lord our God the Almighty reigns. Let us rejoice and exult and give God the glory.   Revelation 19:5-7

Worship God with me, and let us exalt God's name together.

Hallelujah! Let us be glad and rejoice!

Be exalted, O God, above the heavens. Let your glory be over all the earth.

Hallelujah! Let us be glad and rejoice! Let the peoples praise you, O God. Let all the peoples praise you. From Psalms 57, 67

Prayers of Adoration

Holy, holy, holy, Lord God of hosts,
Heaven and earth are full of your glory;
Glory be to you. O Lord most high. **Amen.** *Sanctus*

Eternal God, the same yesterday, today and forever; you are glorious in holiness, full of love and compassion, abounding in grace and truth. All your works praise you in all places and at all times. We worship you. Praise be to you, O God. **Amen.**

Worthy are you, O God, to receive glory and honor and power; for you created all things and by your will they were created and existed. Great and wonderful are your deeds. Just and true are your ways. O Ruler of the ages, we stand in awe and glorify your name. You alone are holy. To you be blessing and honor and glory and might forever and ever. **Amen.**

Almighty God, the creator of all life and being, the fount of all goodness and beauty, the source of truth and love: hallowed be your name. To you be dominion, power, and glory forever and ever. **Amen.**

Eternal God, Creator, Christ, and Holy Spirit, we join with your whole creation in giving you praise. We sing holy, holy, holy, for there is no one beside you. You are in all, beneath all, and beyond all. You were and are and ever-more shall be. Praise be to you, eternal God. **Amen.**

All praise be to you, O God!
We honor your power and magnify your goodness. We sing of your righteousness and tell of your salvation from day to day.
Thank you, God, thank you.
Praise be to you, O God. Amen.

Glory to God, the Creator, and to Christ, the Redeemer, and to the Holy Spirit, the Living Presence:
As it was in the beginning, is now, and ever will be, world without end. Amen.

Glory be to you, Creator God, giver of life and love, who sent Christ into the world to declare your good news of liberation.
Glory be to you, O Christ, who has brought life and freedom to light through the gospel.
Glory be to you, O Holy Spirit, who lives within us, giving to us the spirit of liberty.
Glory be to you, Three in One, One in Three, Creator, Christ, and Holy Spirit! We praise you; we bless you; we thank you. Glory be to you. Amen.

Worthy of praise from every mouth, of confession from every tongue, of worship from every creature, is your glorious name, O God:
Who created the world by your grace and in your compassion saved the world.
To you, O God, ten thousand times ten thousand bow down and adore you, singing and praising without ceasing, saying:

Holy, holy, holy, Lord God of hosts; heaven and earth are full of your praises. Hosanna in the highest. Amen.

Worthy are you, O God, to receive glory and honor and power,
For you created all things, and by your will they existed and were created.
Great and wonderful are your deeds, O God the Almighty!
Just and true are your ways, O Ruler of the ages! To you be honor and glory, dominion and power, now and forever and ever, world without end. Amen.

Let us praise God.
We will continually praise God. Glory to God in the highest and on earth peace among all peoples. Amen.

Eternal God, all praise and honor and glory belong to you.
We praise you for your goodness. We praise you for your compassion and unfailing faithfulness.
We praise you that you are always near; mighty, yet accessible; unknowable, yet known in Jesus Christ.
Let all the earth and all its creatures praise you in all ways. Amen.

We praise you, our God,
For your love revealed to us in Jesus Christ and brought near to us by your Holy Spirit.
We praise you, our God,
For bringing your people from bondage into freedom and making of them one body in Christ.
We praise you, our God,
For calling us to this place of prayer. Make our worship worthy of your love toward us, and having wor-

shiped here help us to go into our several worlds to
be good ministers of that same love. Amen.

Words of Invitation and Promise

Wait for God; be strong, and let your heart take courage;
wait for God.   Psalm 27:14

"Be still, and know that I am God! I am exalted among the
nations, I am exalted in the earth." The God of hosts is
with us; the God of Jacob is our refuge.   Psalm 46:10-11

For God, the Holy One of Israel, has said: "In returning
and rest you shall be saved; in quietness and in trust shall
be your strength."   Isaiah 30:15

Have you not known? Have you not heard? God, the everlasting one, is the Creator of the ends of the earth. God
does not faint or grow weary; God's understanding is
unsearchable. God gives power to the faint, and strength-
ens the powerless. Even youths will faint and be weary,
and the young will fall exhausted; but those who wait for
God shall renew their strength. They shall mount up with
wings like eagles, they shall run and not be weary, they
shall walk and not faint.   Isaiah 40:28-31

Return to God, for your God is gracious and merciful,
slow to anger, and abounding in steadfast love. Joel 2:13

Jesus said, "Come to me, all you that are weary and are
carrying heavy burdens, and I will give you rest. Take my
yoke upon you, and learn from me; for I am gentle and

humble in heart, and you will find rest for your souls. For
my yoke is easy, and my burden is light.''

Matthew 11:28-30

Jesus said, ''Where two or three are gathered in my name,
I am there among them.'' Matthew 18:20

Jesus said, ''Believe me, the hour is coming, and is now
here, when the true worshipers will worship the Creator in
spirit and truth. God is spirit, and those who worship God
must worship in spirit and truth.'' John 4:21,23-24

In everything by prayer and supplication with thanksgiving
let your requests be made known to God. And the peace of
God, which surpasses all understanding, will guard your
hearts and your minds in Christ Jesus. Philippians 4:6-7

Whatever is true, whatever is honorable, whatever is just,
whatever is pure, whatever is pleasing, whatever is commendable, if there is any excellence and if there is anything worthy of praise, think about these things. Keep on
doing the things that you have learned and received and
heard and seen, and the God of peace will be with you.

Philippians 4:8-9

Draw near to God, and God will draw near to you. Humble yourselves before God, and you will be exalted.

James 4:8,10

Jesus said, ''Listen! I am standing at the door, knocking;
if you hear my voice and open the door, I will come in to
you and eat with you, and you with me.'' Revelation 3:20

See, the home of God is among mortals. God will dwell
with them as their God; they will be God's peoples.

Revelation 21:3

The Spirit and the bride say, "Come."
Let everyone who hears say, "Come."
Let everyone who is thirsty come.
Let anyone who wishes take the water of life as a gift.

Revelation 22:17

Make a joyful noise to God, all the earth. Worship God with gladness; come into God's presence with singing.
Know that the Lord is God; we are made by God and we belong to God; we are God's people and the sheep of God's pasture.
Enter God's gates with thanksgiving, and God's courts with praise. Give thanks, bless God's name.
For God is good, God's steadfast love endures forever, and God's faithfulness to all generations. Glory be to God the Creator, and to Christ, and to the Holy Spirit, as it was in the beginning, is now, and ever shall be, world without end. Amen.

Psalm 100, Doxology

Prayers of Invocation

We desire your presence with us, O God. Still our restless spirits, that with quiet minds and reverent hearts we may hear your voice and worthily worship you. **Amen.**

God of love and truth, liberate us from cold hearts and wandering minds when we seek to come near to you, that with firm convictions and kindled affections we may worship you in love and truth. **Amen.**

Help us in this time of worship to be still and know that you are God. In quietness we would hear your voice calling us away from the discordant noises of the everyday world, that our spirits might be renewed and we may go back into the world to minister in your name. **Amen.**

We hear you knocking, O God, as you stand outside the locked doors of our hearts, waiting and wanting to enter. Help us to throw open those doors, that in this time of worship you may come in as a living presence and we may offer to you our praise and thanksgiving. **Amen.**

Eternal God, who exists from eternity to eternity, and is not at one time or one place because all times and all places are in you, we stand before you frail and mortal. But blessed are you, O God of the universe, for you have made us in your own image and breathed into us your spirit. From our small space and limited time we dare to lift our spirits beyond all time and space to you, the eternal One, to give praise and thanksgiving. We beseech you that in this hour of worship you will come and renew within us an energizing sense of your eternal presence. **Amen.**

As we worship you, O God, unstop our ears, that we might hear your word. Sweep the cobwebs from our minds, that we may receive your truth. Strengthen our wills, that we may become your true disciples. And warm our hearts, that we may receive a full measure of your love. **Amen.**

Sovereign God, your power and your glory are beyond our understanding; your mercy is vast and your tenderness without end. Look in love upon us assembled in this house of prayer, and show your mercy and loving-kindness to all throughout the world who are united with us in thanksgiving and praise. Yours is the glory, and the power, and the honor, now and for all ages. **Amen.**

Armenian Liturgy, adapted

Eternal God, Creator and Ruler of the world, we come with humility and gratitude as we gather to seek your presence. Inspire, refresh, and revive us, that we may truly worship you with hymns, prayers, words, and deeds. **Amen.**

Almighty God, who has given us grace at this time with one accord to make our common supplication to you, and who has promised that when two or three are gathered together in Christ's name you will be in the midst of them: Fulfill now the desires and petitions of your servants as may be best for us; granting us in this world knowledge of your truth, and in the world to come life everlasting. **Amen.**   John Chrysostom, 345–407, adapted

Help us, O God, who are gathered in this place to present ourselves as living sacrifices, holy and acceptable to you. **Amen.**

Bless us as we worship you. Of your goodness, give us; with your love, inspire us; by your Spirit, guide us; in your mercy, receive us, now and always. **Amen.**

An ancient prayer, adapted

We thank you, O God, for these special moments when we can bring to you our innermost thoughts and prayers. Deepen our spirits; keep our minds alert; may we ever be attentive to that still, small voice which can speak to us of your love and care. **Amen.**

Parent God, in this time of worship we come to you as children eager to learn your truth. Teach us through your word. Mold us according to your will. Take our hands and lead us into the paths of right living. Cause our hearts to pound and our veins to surge with the power of new life. Help us to love you more and more, even as you love us. **Amen.**

Creator God who makes light to shine out of darkness, shine into our hearts that we may truly praise you. Awaken us to your goodness and grace and accept our worship, that we may through the liberating grace that you offer to us become children of light. **Amen.**

You have taught us, O God, that in returning and rest we shall be saved, and in quietness and confidence we shall find our strength. In this time of stillness come to us, fill us with your Spirit, and make your presence known to us, that we may find new life in you. **Amen.**

Gracious God, who gave the sun to illumine the day and the moon and stars to shine by night, enlighten us in this hour of worship that we may become children of light. May the light that you give us so shine before others that they give you the glory. **Amen.**

Gracious God, open our lips, that we may give you the praise due you and offer to you our thanks for your enduring goodness. **Amen.**

This is the time and this is the place. We wait for you, God, to come to us:
**To change our minds,
To remold our lives,
To fill us with hope.**

All: **Here and now, in this place and at this time, come to us, O God. Amen.**

Hear, O God, our voices. Let your ear be attentive to our confessions and supplications.
We wait for you, O God.
Hope in God. For with God there is steadfast love and great power to redeem.
We wait for you, O God. Amen.

Gracious God, open our lips,
That our mouths may show forth your praise.
Gracious God, open our minds,
That our thoughts may be formed by you.
Gracious God, open our hearts,
That we may receive the fullness of your grace.
Be pleased, gracious God, to grant that in this hour of worship we may find wholeness,
By becoming whole in you. Amen.

Eternal God, in this quiet hour we seek you. From the day's discordant noises, from the fret and fever of the world's business, from the praise and blame of those around us, from the confused thoughts and vain imaginations of our minds, we now turn to search out the quietness of your presence.
Help us to listen for the still, small voice, that we may know a great sense of your glory and power. Amen.

Loving God, you are far off yet ever near, and you have promised that if we seek you with our whole heart, we shall find you. Help us as we seek.
Renew a right spirit within us, and help us to follow that way which leads to a never-ending and always-loving relationship with you. Amen.

In this time of worship, O God, direct and control our thoughts that we may think only of you. Grant us:

To adore you, as we remember your glory; to be penitent, as we remember your holiness; to be thankful, as we remember your love. Amen.

Confession

Calls to Confession

God said, ''If my people who are called by my name humble themselves, pray, seek my face, and turn from their wicked ways, then I will hear and forgive their sin and heal their land.''   2 Chronicles 7:14

Yield yourselves to God and come to the sanctuary. For your God is gracious and merciful, and will not turn away from you, if you return.   2 Chronicles 30:8-9

Taste and see that God is good; happy are those who take refuge in God. Depart from evil, and do good; seek peace, and pursue it. The eyes of God are on the righteous, and God's ears are open to their cry. God is near to the brokenhearted, and saves the crushed in spirit. None of those who take refuge in God will be condemned.

Psalm 34:8,14-15,18,22

The sacrifice acceptable to God is a broken spirit; a broken and contrite heart, O God, you will not despise.

Psalm 51:17

Bless God, who forgives all your iniquity, who heals all your diseases, who redeems your life, who crowns you with steadfast love and mercy, who satisfies you with good as long as you live so that your youth is renewed like the eagle's.   Psalm 103:2-5

God is gracious and merciful, slow to anger and abounding in steadfast love. God is good to all, and God's compassion is over all that has been made.   Psalm 145:8-9

Though your sins are like scarlet, they shall be like snow; though they are red like crimson, they shall become like wool.   Isaiah 1:18

Let the wicked forsake their way, and the unrighteous their thoughts; let them return to God, that God may have mercy upon them, for God will abundantly pardon.   Isaiah 55:7

Return to God with all your heart. Rend your hearts and not your clothing. Return to God, for your God is gracious and merciful, slow to anger, and abounding in steadfast love.   Joel 2:12-13

With what shall I come before God? God has told you, O mortal, what is good; and what does God require of you but to do justice, and to love kindness, and to walk humbly with your God?   Micah 6:6,8

The prodigal said, ''I will get up and go to my father, and I will say to him, 'Father, I have sinned against heaven and before you; I am no longer worthy to be called your child.' ''   Luke 15:18

I appeal to you, brothers and sisters, by the mercies of God, to present your bodies as a living sacrifice, holy and acceptable to God, which is your spiritual worship. Do not

be conformed to this world, but be transformed by the renewing of your minds, so that you may discern what is the will of God—what is good and acceptable and perfect.
Romans 12:1-2

You know what time it is, how it is now the moment for you to wake from sleep. For salvation is nearer to us now than when we became believers; the night is far gone, the day is near. Let us then lay aside the works of darkness and put on the armor of light. Romans 13:11-12

Who shall ascend the hill of God? And who shall stand in that holy place?
Those who have clean hands and pure hearts, who do not lift up their souls to what is false, who do not swear deceitfully.
They will receive blessing from God, and vindication from the God of their salvation.
Such is the company of those who seek God, who seek the face of the God of Jacob. Psalm 24:3-6

God is light and in God there is no darkness at all. If we say we have fellowship with God while we are walking in darkness, we lie and do not do what is true; but if we walk in the light as God is in the light, we have fellowship with one another, and the blood of Jesus cleanses us from all sin.
If we say that we have no sin, we deceive ourselves, and the truth is not in us. If we confess our sins, God who is faithful and just will forgive us our sins and cleanse us from all unrighteousness. 1 John 1:5-9

Since we have a great high priest, Jesus Christ, let us hold fast to our confession. For we do not have a high priest who is unable to sympathize with our weaknesses, but we have one who in every respect has been tested as we are, yet without sin.

Let us therefore approach the throne of grace with boldness, so that we may receive mercy and find grace to help in the time of need. Hebrews 4:14-16

Those who desire life and desire to see good days, let them keep their tongues from evil and their lips from speaking deceit; let them turn away from evil and do good; let them seek peace and pursue it.

For the eyes of God are on the righteous, and God's ears are open to their prayer. 1 Peter 3:10-12

The good news is this: Christ came into the world to save sinners.

Let us therefore open ourselves to Christ's saving love as we humbly confess our sins, and in faith receive cleansing. 1 Timothy 1:15

Prayers of Confession

Almighty and most merciful God, we have erred and strayed from your ways like lost sheep. We have followed too much the devices and desire of our own hearts. We have offended against your holy laws. We have left undone those things which we ought to have done; and we have done those things which we ought not to have done; and there is no health in us. Have mercy, O God, upon us. Spare those who confess their faults. Restore those who are penitent, according to the promises declared to humankind in Christ Jesus. And grant, O most merciful God, for Christ's sake, that we may hereafter live a godly, righteous, and sober life, to the glory of your holy name. **Amen.**   A General Confession

Merciful God, we confess that we have been unfaithful to you and unloving to those around us. When those in need have cried out for help, we have turned our backs upon them, and in so doing have shut the doors of our hearts to your love for them through us. Forgive us. **Amen.**

Eternal God, who by your love has made us, through your love has kept us, and in your love would make us to be wholly in accordance with your holy will, we humbly confess that we have not loved you with all our heart and soul and mind and strength, and that we have not loved our neighbors as Christ loves them and us. We have resisted your Spirit and gone our own ways. Forgive what we have been and help us to change what we are. By your Spirit direct what we shall be, that your image may come into full glory in us and in all people. **Amen.**

Sovereign God, we confess that we have not lived the life of which we are capable. We have gifts which we have not used and gifts we have misused. We have not loved you above all lesser loves, and we have failed to love our neighbor as ourselves. Have mercy and forgive us, and lift us to a nobler level of living. **Amen.**

Eternal God, we know you would not love us for long, except that your love is unchanging. Look upon us with a sense of humor, for even when we are confessing our sin, we put into words the petty while leaving the weighty unspoken. Lift from us the burden of that which does not matter, and free us from the bewildering array of problems of our own making. Help us to awaken to the reality that in Jesus Christ our sin is forgiven, and that in his way of love we are truly free. **Amen.**

The prodigal said, "I will get up and go to my father, and I will say to him, 'Father, I have sinned against heaven and before you; I am no longer worthy to be called your child.'" Let us, like the prodigal, come to our divine Parent, and seek forgiveness for our sin. Let us pray:

Most merciful God, we bow before you and confess that like foolish children we have rebelled against you and our own true home. We have wandered far away, seeking gratification for our desires. We have wasted your good gifts in self-indulgent living. We have sought sustenance amidst alien places. Forgive us: cleanse us, that by your forgiving love we are able to find the way back to our true home. Amen.

Have mercy upon us, O God, according to your steadfast love;
According to your abundant mercy blot out our transgressions.
Wash us thoroughly from our iniquity,
And cleanse us from our sin.
For we know our transgressions,
And our sin is ever before us.
Against you, you alone, have we sinned,
And done what is evil in your sight,
So that you are justified in your sentence,
And blameless when you pass judgment.
Create in us clean hearts, O God,
And put a new and right spirit within us.
Do not cast us away from your presence,

And do not take your Holy Spirit from us.
Restore to us the joy of your salvation,
And sustain in us a willing spirit. Amen.

Psalm 51:1-4,10-12

O God, our God, great, eternal, wonderful in glory, the hope of all who call out to you:
Cleanse us from our sins, and from every thought displeasing to you. Cleanse our souls and bodies, our hearts and consciences, that with pure hearts and clear minds, with perfected love and calm hope, we may venture confidently and fearlessly to pray to you. Amen. An ancient collect, adapted

Loving God, whose tender mercies are over all your works, and whose love reaches out to all who bow before you in humble repentance, we come to you confessing that we have sinned in thought, word and deed. We seek your forgiveness: For every defiling thought that our minds have harbored,
Forgive us.
For every ill word spoken hastily or in dark passion,
Forgive us.
For every failure in self-control,
Forgive us.
For loitering feet and procrastinating will,
Forgive us.
For every stumbling block by deed or example we have set in another's way,
Forgive us.
For every lost opportunity to do good,
Forgive us, and grant that your Spirit will give us the victory over these and all other sinful ways. Amen.

We cannot truly praise God unless we humble ourselves and come to God confessing our sin and asking for forgiveness. Let us therefore acknowledge our sinfulness and bow before God in penitent prayer.

The people silently confess their sins, after which the worship leader says:

Forgiving God, hear the confessions of your people. Be pleased to pardon their iniquities and cause them henceforth to walk in paths of your choosing. **Amen.**

God of mercy, we acknowledge that you have called us to follow you, yet so often we have failed in our commitment to be loyal disciples.

Help us once again to hear your call and follow you.
We confess that we have loved ourselves too much and others too little.

Help us to hear and live by your commandment that we should love you with heart and mind and soul and our neighbor as ourselves.

All: **Forgive us, God of mercy, and help us find our true calling in your service. Amen.**

Words of Assurance of Forgiveness

God is near to the brokenhearted, and saves the crushed in spirit. None of those who take refuge in God will be condemned. Psalm 34:18,22

God is near to all who call, to all who call in truth. God hears their cry and saves them. Psalm 145:18-19

I, I am God, and besides me is no savior. I, I am God who blots out your transgression for my own sake, and I will not remember your sins. Isaiah 43:11,25

The steadfast love of God never ceases; God's mercies never come to an end. They are new every morning; great is God's faithfulness.   Lamentations 3:22-23

Jesus said, "Come to me, all you that are weary and carrying heavy burdens, and I will give you rest."
                                        Matthew 11:28

Since we are justified by faith, we have peace with God through Jesus Christ. There is therefore no condemnation for those who are in Christ.   Romans 5:1; 8:1

The saying is sure and worthy of full acceptance, that Christ Jesus came into the world to save sinners. 1 Timothy 1:15

This is the message we have heard from God and proclaim to you, that God is light and in God there is no darkness at all. If we walk in the light as God is in the light, we have fellowship with one another, and the blood of Jesus cleanses us from all sin.   1 John 1:5,7

If we confess our sins, God who is faithful and just will forgive us our sins and cleanse us from all unrighteousness.   1 John 1:9

If anyone does sin, we have an advocate with God, Jesus Christ the righteous; and he is the atoning sacrifice for our sins, and not for ours only but also for the sins of the whole world.   1 John 2:1-2

Ministry of the Word

Prayers Before the Sermon

O Jesus Christ, who fed the multitudes upon the hillside, feed us now with your Word, that we too may be filled. **Amen.**

God of truth, who desires that we live by your truth, may the words spoken this day take root within the hearts of all who hear and be brought to fruition in true servanthood in the world. **Amen.**

Prepare our minds and hearts, O God, that through your Word, read and proclaimed, Christ may come to dwell within us, and ever rule over our thoughts and affections as Lord of our lives. **Amen.**

May your Word read and proclaimed this day be for us a lamp upon the way and a light upon the path, that we may go forth from this place of worship confident that we are walking with you. **Amen.**

Eternal God, take the human words which are about to be spoken and make of them a fitting channel for your holy Word. **Amen.**

Creator God, who commanded the light to shine out of darkness, through your Word enter into our hearts, that we may become for you lights to the world. **Amen.**

Spirit of Truth, as we turn to your Word let the light of your countenance be upon us, that we may come to know more fully the one who is the way, the truth, and the life, even Christ Jesus, our Lord. **Amen.**

O God, may the Word that is read and spoken become through us a liberating word to all who are in bondage to sin, sickness, or poverty, and who long for freedom. **Amen.**

May the words of my mouth,
And the meditations of our hearts be acceptable to you, our rock and our redeemer. Amen.

Affirmations of Faith

The Apostles' Creed

I believe in God the Father Almighty, maker of heaven and earth:

And in Jesus Christ his only Son our Lord: who was conceived by the Holy Spirit, born of the Virgin Mary, suffered under Pontius Pilate, was crucified, dead and buried. The third day he rose again from the dead. He ascended into heaven, and sits on the right hand of God the Father Almighty. From thence he shall come to judge the living and the dead.

I believe in the Holy Spirit; the holy catholic church; the communion of saints; the forgiveness of sins; the resurrection of the body; and the life everlasting.

Salem Church Covenant

We covenant with the Lord and with one another and do bind ourselves in the presence of God to walk in all his ways as he is pleased to reveal himself to us in his blessed word of truth.

Scriptural Affirmations

God is spirit, and those who worship must worship in spirit and truth. God is light and in God is no darkness at all. God is love and those who abide in love abide in God, and God abides in them. There is no fear in love, but perfect love casts out fear. We love because God first loved us. The commandment which we have from God is this: those who love God must love their brothers and sisters also. Love is patient; love is kind; love is not envious or boastful or arrogant or rude. It does not insist on its own way. It bears all things, believes all things, hopes all things, endures all things. Love never ends. So then we are debtors, not to the flesh, to live according to the flesh, but we received the spirit of adoption. Therefore, being of good courage, we walk by faith, not by sight, and we make it our aim to please God. For we know that all things work together for good for those who love God, who are called according to God's purpose.

Where the Spirit of God is, there is the one true church, apostolic and universal, whose faith let us now reverently and sincerely declare:

We believe that God is spirit, and those who worship must worship in spirit and truth.

We believe that God is light, and if we walk in the light as God is in the light, we have fellowship with one another.

We believe that God is love, and everyone who loves is born of God and knows God.

We believe that Jesus Christ is the Son of God, and that in Christ God has given us eternal life. Whoever has the Son has life.

We believe that if we confess our sin God, who is faithful and just, will forgive our sins and cleanse us from all unrighteousness.

We believe that though the world passes away the one who does the will of God abides forever.

Ministry of the Table

Prayers of Petition

We bow before you, Creator God, from whom the whole family in heaven and earth is named, that you may grant us, according to the riches of your glory, to be strength-

ened in the inner person with might by your Spirit, that Christ may dwell in our hearts by faith; that we, being rooted and grounded in love, may be able to know and comprehend with all the saints what is the breadth, and depth, and height, and to know the love of Christ, which passes all knowledge, that we might be filled with all the fullness of God. **Amen.** A General Petition
Ephesians 3:14-19

All-merciful God, who of your great love to all peoples gave Jesus Christ to die for us, grant that through his cross our sins may be put away and remembered no more; and that, cleansed by his blood and mindful of his sufferings, we may take up our cross daily and follow him in newness of life, until we come to his eternal kingdom. **Amen.**

Give us wisdom, O Christ, to build our house upon the rock, and not upon the sand; that should the floods of doubt, rains of affliction, and winds of loneliness beat upon us, we may not fall because we are founded on the rock, even you, O Christ. **Amen.**

Give us wisdom, give us courage for the living of these days; but above all else give us love, that we may love our neighbors, not only as we love ourselves, but as you love them. **Amen.**

Grant us, O God, to know that which is worth knowing, and to esteem that which to you is precious. Help us to discriminate between that which lasts and the ever-changing, and above all to seek the good pleasure of your will. **Amen.**

Give us strength, gracious God, to serve you as you deserve to be served; to give and not count the cost; to fight and not heed the wounds; to labor and ask for no reward save that of knowing that we do what is pleasing to you. **Amen.**

O God, who has made of one blood all people to dwell on the face of the earth, and did send Jesus Christ to preach peace to them that are afar off, and to them that are near at hand: grant that all peoples of the world may seek after you and find you, and hasten, O God, the fulfillment of your promise to pour out your Spirit upon all flesh; through Jesus Christ our Lord. **Amen.**

Bishop Cotton of Calcutta, 1813–1866; adapted

Save us, O Christ, from the error of only admiring you instead of being willing to follow you. **Amen.**

God of love, who has made our hearts restless until they find their rest in you, help us to so live your love among others that they may see your love in us and enter into a loving relationship with you. **Amen.**

Almighty God, who has given us grace at this time with one accord to make our common petitions to you, and who has promised that where two or three are gathered together in your name you will grant their requests; fulfill the desires of your servants as may be most expedient for them, granting us in this world knowledge of your truth, and in the world to come life eternal. **Amen.**

Loving God, take from us the contemptuous pride which bruises the self-respect of our brothers and sisters, and when our brothers and sisters are bent down with loads too heavy to bear, help us to lift their burdens and carry them the extra mile. **Amen.**

Strong Deliverer, we come to you seeking freedom to live as you would have us live. Hear us as we bring our petitions to you and give us strength to walk in your way. From idleness and weakness of purpose, from indifference, carelessness, and insincerity,

Deliver us, Gracious God, and grant us healing.

From despondency and lack of faith, from cowardice and self-conceit,

Deliver us, Gracious God, and grant us healing.

From dishonesty, extravagance, and debt, and from all frailty of the flesh,

Deliver us, Gracious God, and grant us healing.

From all temptation to put pleasure above duty, and all injustice to others,

Deliver us, Gracious God, and grant us healing.

In times of ignorance and perplexity, in times of confusion and discord,

Help us, Gracious God, and grant us healing. Amen.

Prayers of Intercession

O God, Creator and Preserver of all, we humbly beseech you for all sorts and conditions of people, that you would be pleased to make your ways known to them, and your saving health to all nations. Especially we pray for the universal church, that it may be so guided and governed by your good Spirit that all who profess and call themselves Christians may be led into the way of truth, and hold the faith in unity of spirit, in the bond of peace, and in righteousness of life. Finally, we commend to your caring goodness all who are in any way afflicted or distressed in mind, body, or circumstance (especially...); that it may please you to comfort and relieve them according to their needs, giving them patience under their sufferings and a happy issue out of all their afflictions. All this we ask for Jesus Christ's sake. **Amen.**

A General Intercession, adapted

God of all might and love, who has given us confidence to come to you with our petitions and intercessions, we bring to you the needs of the world. In this time of global tension, when your children are taught to hate and kill one another, we pray for your Spirit to bring peace and reconciliation to all. Lead all people and agencies committed to international understanding to turn to the teachings of Jesus Christ for guidance into the way of peace, and inspire the leaders of all nations to prepare a way by which all peoples may walk together as one family under you. **Amen.**

Merciful God, who has promised that nothing can separate us from your love in Christ Jesus, be with us as we come to you with our needs and desires. If we mourn, comfort us; if we are sick, heal us; if we despair, encourage us; if we fall, strengthen us; and if we are unhappy, bring us joy. Give the full measure of your bounty to those not present among us this day according to their needs (especially...); and give us sensitivity and strength to minister in your name and with your Spirit to others in need. **Amen.**

Parent of all, we pray for the children of the world. You who have a special love for these little ones, deepen our concern for them. Give us grace to become your instruments in meeting their needs. Help us to feed the hungry, clothe the naked, teach the unlearned, befriend the lonely, give shelter to the homeless. Through these ministries may these your little ones come to know and love you. We pray in the name of Jesus, who loved children and said, "Let them come to me." **Amen.**

We beseech you, O God, to hear our prayers for your church. Fill it with truth and peace. Where it is corrupt, purify it; where it is in error, correct it; where it is slow to speak and act, move it by your wisdom and power; where it is rejected, help it to understand; where it is misjudged, help it not to bring judgment; where it is divided, unite it; and whether it is right or wrong, love it at all times for the sake of Jesus Christ. **Amen.**

All powerful God, Creator and Ruler of the world and its peoples, we pray that peace will increase in our time. May it please you to guide the leaders of every land. Help them to find the ways whereby all nations can be led into those paths which bring them to that common accord wherein they can live in friendship one with another. **Amen.**

Let us pray for our community, that selfish interest might give way to selfless service, that the walls which keep people apart might come down, and that we might come to live together in peace and equality.
(Silence)

Lord of Life, who desires that all persons live in peace with their neighbors and work together for the common good, grant that in this community the unredeemed power of greed may be uprooted, the walls of division be shattered, and the bonds that unite us be strengthened, that we may all live together in peace: the rich and the poor, the strong and the weak, the healthy and the sick, the young and the old. Amen.

Let us pray for the church universal and for this congregation, that as a family chosen by God we may become an instrument of God's will in this place and throughout the world.

(Silence)

Lord of the church, who has called us and made us one people, we pray for the insight, courage, power, and love to perform your work and witness in our community and the world. Amen.

Gracious God, who in Jesus Christ has taught us to pray, so guide us by your Holy Spirit that our prayers for others will be in accord with your will and may show forth your steadfast love. Let us pray for the world:

God of all the worlds that are, we pray for the whole creation: tame unruly power; crush every tyranny; rebuke injustice; bring liberation to all who are oppressed; that all your children may enjoy this good world which you have made and glory in the salvation brought by Jesus Christ. Amen.

Let us pray for peace:

Eternal God, speed the day when wars are ended and peace reigns throughout the whole world, and all your children are reconciled one with another and with you. Amen.

God wills that all persons be made whole in body, mind, and spirit. Let us pray for those whose minds are troubled, whose bodies are filled with pain, and whose spirits are broken.

Merciful God, who bears the pain of the world, look with compassion upon those whose lives are broken, troubled, or filled with pain (especially. . .), that

they may be strengthened by your presence and ministered to by your grace. Amen.

Let us pray for one another, that at home, at school, at leisure, and at work we might live as people who have been made new in Jesus Christ.
(Silence)
You, O God, have promised to be with us as we seek to live according to our calling in Christ Jesus; strengthen, encourage, rebuke, and comfort us as we endeavor to walk faithfully in the ways Jesus taught us. Amen.

The worship leader may present the requests for prayer, or call for such requests from the congregation. After each request the minister prays as follows or in his or her words:
Merciful God, we bring before you *(here the request is repeated)*. Be pleased to grant our petition in accordance with your will. **Amen.**

Offertory Sentences

Give liberally and be ungrudging when you do so, for on this account God will bless you in all your work and in all that you undertake. Deuteronomy 15:10

Open your hand to the poor and needy neighbor in your land. Deuteronomy 15:11

All shall give as they are able, according to the blessing of God that has been given to you. Deuteronomy 16:17

Ascribe to God glory! Bring an offering, and come into God's courts. Psalm 96:8

Honor God with your substance and with the first fruits of all your produce.   Proverbs 3:9

Bring the full tithe into the storehouse.   Malachi 3:10

On entering the house, the wise men saw the child with Mary his mother; and they knelt down and paid him homage. Then, opening their treasure chests, they offered him gifts of gold, frankincense, and myrrh.   Matthew 2:11

When you are offering your gift at the altar, if you remember that your brother or sister has something against you, leave your gift there before the altar and go; first be reconciled to your brother or sister, and then come and offer your gift.   Matthew 5:23-24

Jesus said, "Do not store up for yourselves treasures on earth, where moth and rust consume and where thieves break in and steal; but store up for yourselves treasures in heaven, where neither moth nor rust consumes and where thieves do not break in and steal. For where your treasure is, there will your heart be also."   Matthew 6:19-21

Freely you have received, freely give.   Matthew 10:8 (KJV)

Jesus said, "Give to the emperor the things that are the emperor's, and to God the things that are God's."
                    Matthew 22:21

Jesus said, "I was hungry and you gave me food. I was thirsty and you gave me something to drink. I was a stranger and you welcomed me. I was naked and you gave me clothing. I was sick and you took care of me. I was in prison and you visited me."   Matthew 25:35-36

Jesus said, "Those who want to save their life will lose it, and those who lose their life for my sake, and for the sake of the gospel, will save it. For what will it profit them to gain the whole world and forfeit their life?" Mark 8:35-36

Jesus said, "If any want to become my followers, let them deny themselves and take up their cross daily and follow me. For those who want to save their life will lose it, and those who lose their life for my sake will save it. What does it profit them if they gain the whole world, but lose or forfeit themselves?" Luke 9:23-25

From everyone to whom much has been given, much will be required; and from the one to whom much has been entrusted, even more will be demanded. Luke 12:48

Whoever is faithful in a very little is faithful also in much. No one can serve two masters; you cannot serve God and wealth. Luke 16:10,13

Remember the words of the Lord Jesus, for he himself said, "It is more blessed to give than to receive." Acts 20:35

We have gifts that differ according to the grace given to us: prophecy, in proportion to faith; ministry, in ministering; the teacher, in teaching; the exhorter, in exhortation; the giver, in generosity; the leader, in diligence; the compassionate, in cheerfulness. Romans 12:6-8

It is required of stewards that they be found trustworthy.
1 Corinthians 4:2

On the first day of every week, each of you is to put something aside and store it up, as you may prosper.
1 Corinthians 16:2 (RSV)

They voluntarily gave according to their means, and even beyond their means, but first they gave themselves to the Lord.   2 Corinthians 8:3,5

You know the generous act of our Lord Jesus Christ, that though he was rich, yet for your sakes he became poor, so that by his poverty you might become rich.

2 Corinthians 8:9

Each of you must give as you have made up your mind, not reluctantly or under compulsion, for God loves a cheerful giver.   2 Corinthians 9:7

Let us not grow weary in doing what is right. Whenever we have an opportunity, let us work for the good of all, and especially for those of the family of faith. Galatians 6:9-10

We are to do good, to be rich in good works, generous, and ready to share, thus storing up for ourselves the treasure of a good foundation for the future, so that we may take hold of the life that really is life. 1 Timothy 6:18-19

Do not neglect to do good and to share what you have, for such sacrifices are pleasing to God.   Hebrews 13:16

How does God's love abide in anyone who has the world's goods and sees a brother or sister in need and yet refuses help? Let us love, not in word or speech, but in truth and action.   1 John 3:17-18

All of you cannot abandon your possessions, but at least you can change your attitude to them. There is a taint in trying to get it all; all-getting separates you from others, but all-giving unites you to them. Believe me, getting it all over and above your simplest needs will be tainted with distress, but giving will be a source of joy.

Francis of Assisi, 1182–1226

From the heart bring forth incense of praise, from the store of a good conscience bring forth the sacrifice of faith, and whatsoever you bring forth kindle it with love. These are the most acceptable offerings to God: mercy, humility, confession, peace, love. It is you that God seeks more than any gift.

Augustine, Bishop of Hippo, 354–430

Teach us, God, to serve you as you deserve; to give and not to count the cost. To labor and not ask for reward, save in the knowledge that we do your will.

Ignatius Loyola, 1491–1556

We give but little when we give our possessions. It is when we give of ourselves that we truly give.

Kahlil Gibran 1883–1931; adapted

Prayers of Dedication

Dedication of Self

We offer and present to you, Redeemer God, ourselves to serve you. Take us as we are and equip us for that service. We are not our own, but yours, bought with a price; therefore claim us as your right, keep us in your charge, use us as you will and when you will, to your glory. **Amen.**

Living God, who has given us life and liberty, enable us to glorify you through faithful service. Take first place in our lives, and forbid, we pray you, that personal ambition or unworthy purposes should tempt us to forget the stewardship that you have given into our hands. **Amen.**

Forbid that we should sit idly by when people around us are hungry, homeless, despondent, or despised, and are crying out for help. Give us the love of Jesus, who ministered to all in need regardless of their station in life. **Amen.**

Living God, take our lives and consecrate them as sanctuaries, that they may become houses of prayer and fit dwelling places for your Spirit. May that same Spirit become through us a light to be carried to those lost amidst their inner darkness. **Amen.**

We know, O God, that we are most truly free when we lose our wills in you; help us to gain this freedom by the daily surrender of our lives to you; through Jesus Christ our Lord. **Amen.**

Thank you, God, for all that you have given us. To you be honor and glory forever. We pray that all your blessings may make us daily more diligent to devote ourselves and all that we have to your glory and to the service of others. **Amen.**

Help us, O God, to hear Christ calling to us through voices of the oppressed, the sick, the imprisoned, those discriminated against because of race, sex, or nationality, and those entangled in the bleak coils of poverty. May we, having heard the call, answer, Send us. **Amen.**

God of truth, open our minds to your truth. Help us not to cling so to the past that we are unwilling to be moved by that which is new. Make us hospitable to the thoughts of others, even when such thoughts call our own positions into question. Help us ever to seek him who is the way, the truth, and the life, Christ Jesus our Lord. **Amen.**

Open our hands to the world, ready to share the benefits we have so bountifully received from you, our God. Transform all inclinations toward greed into a spirit of generosity. Help us to use our possessions wisely and not for ourselves alone, that they may minister to others and give glory to you. **Amen.**

Give us grateful hearts, O God, for all your mercies to us, and make us ever mindful of the needs of others, that we may serve them and, through them, serve you. **Amen.**

Thank you, God, for the blessings that we receive as we worship you. Deepen within us the wells of your Spirit, that they may overflow to those around us and give us sustenance for our daily life. **Amen.**

Dedication of Gifts

Be pleased, O God, to accept this offering of our money as a symbol of our love and devotion to you. Give to those who expend it grace to use it wisely for the extension of your dominion in this place and throughout the world. **Amen.**

We pray, O God, that these gifts be accepted as the symbols of our lives. For as we dedicate these gifts, so do we consecrate our lives to your service. **Amen.**

Gracious God, who gave Jesus Christ and who with him has given so freely to us, receive these our offerings and enable us, with all our gifts, so to yield ourselves to you that with body, mind, and spirit we may truly and freely serve you, for in that service we find our deepest joy. **Amen.**

Loving God, giver of every good and perfect gift, in gratitude we give these gifts to you. With them, we consecrate ourselves to your service. Use us and that which we have given for your work in the world, that both gift and giver may be a blessing to those who receive. **Amen.**

Receive these our offerings and bless their use, that they may find manifold avenues of service in this place and throughout the world. **Amen.**

Gracious God, help us to be cheerful givers, that in giving we may find joy, and having found joy, go forth to spread it abroad, that the world might become a more joyful place in which to live. **Amen.**

Giving God, from whom we have received so much, be pleased to accept these gifts.
Bless them and use them to promote peace and goodwill in this place and throughout the world, for the sake of Christ who loved us and gave himself for us. Amen.

Creator God, by whose will the world came into being and who has given to us life and sustenance: with thankful hearts we praise you for your goodness and thank you for your bounty.
As a token of our thankfulness we bring these gifts to you. Use them and us as seems best to you for the

renewal of your creation, both in our lives and throughout the world. Amen.

Prayers of Dedication when the Lord's Supper is Observed

To your table we bring gifts of money, bread, and wine, and with these gifts we offer ourselves. Consecrate each to your service. **Amen.**

Holy God, Creator, Redeemer, and Sovereign, we offer to you this bread and wine, thanking you for the food you have given us out of earth and sea, and we present to you our gifts, blessing you for the skill and strength to do our daily work; and together with them we offer ourselves, asking you to strengthen and sanctify us by your Holy Spirit, that all our meals may be sacraments, our work worship, and our bodies a living sacrifice, holy and acceptable to you. **Amen.**

To your table, Gracious Christ, we bring money.
  Consecrate this money to your mission in this place and throughout the world.
To your table, Gracious Christ, we bring bread and wine.
  Consecrate this common bread and wine to make of them the means whereby we may once again receive you into our lives.
To your table, Gracious Christ, we bring ourselves.
  Consecrate us and make each of us a living sacrifice, holy and acceptable to you. Amen.

We bring these gifts to you, our God, and with them we bring ourselves.
  Be pleased to accept all that we have brought. May the money be used in the proclamation of the good

news in this place and beyond. May the bread and wine be a reminder that Christ lives and can come to abide with us as our constant companion and friend. And may we willingly offer ourselves as tokens of Christ's presence in our midst. Amen.

Invitation to Communion

While they were eating, Jesus took a loaf of bread, and after blessing it he broke it, gave it to them, and said, "Take; this is my body." Then he took a cup, and after giving thanks he gave it to them, and all of them drank from it. He said, "This is my blood of the covenant, which is poured out for many. Truly I tell you, I will never again drink of the fruit of the vine until that day when I drink it new in the kingdom of God." When they had sung a hymn, they went out to the Mount of Olives.

Mark 14:22-26

When the hour (for the Passover meal) came, Jesus took his place at the table, and the apostles with him. He said to them, "I have eagerly desired to eat this Passover with you before I suffer; for I tell you, I will not eat it until it is fulfilled in the kingdom of God." Then he took a cup, and after giving thanks he said, "Take this and divide it among yourselves; for I tell you that from now on I will not drink of the fruit of the vine until the kingdom of God comes." Then he took a loaf of bread, and when he had given thanks, he broke it and gave it to them, saying, "This is my body, which is given for you. Do this in remembrance of me." And he did the same with the cup after supper, saying, "This cup that is poured out for you is the new covenant in my blood."

Luke 22:14-20

When Jesus was at the table with the two men of Emmaus, he took bread, blessed and broke it, and gave it to them. Then their eyes were opened, and they recognized him; and he vanished from their sight. They said to each other, "Were not our hearts burning within us while he was talking to us on the road, while he was opening the scriptures to us?" That same hour they got up and returned to Jerusalem; and they found the eleven and their companions gathered together. Then they told what had happened on the road, and how he had been made known to them in the breaking of the bread. While they were talking about this, Jesus himself stood among them and said, "Peace be with you." Luke 24:30-33,35-36

Jesus said, "I am the bread of life. Whoever comes to me will never be hungry, and whoever believes in me will never be thirsty." John 6:35

Jesus said, "Very truly, I tell you, unless you eat my flesh and drink my blood, you have no life in you. Those who eat my flesh and drink my blood have eternal life; they abide in me and I in them." John 6:53-54,56

Jesus said, "This is the bread that came down from heaven. The one who eats this bread will live forever." John 6:58

The cup of blessing that we bless, is it not a sharing in the blood of Christ? Because there is one bread, we who are many are one body, for we all partake of the one bread. 1 Corinthians 10:16-17

Whether you eat or drink, or whatever you do, do everything for the glory of God. 1 Corinthians 10:31

Whoever eats the bread or drinks the cup of the Lord in an unworthy manner will be answerable for the body and blood of the Lord. Examine yourselves, and only then eat of the bread and drink of the cup. For all who eat and drink without discerning the Lord's body, eat and drink judgment against themselves. 1 Corinthians 11:27-29

Beloved, let us love one another, because love is from God; everyone who loves is born of God and knows God.
1 John 4:7

Jesus said, "Listen! I am standing at the door, knocking; if you hear my voice and open the door, I will come in to you and eat with you, and you with me." Revelation 3:20

Taste and see that God is good.
Happy are those who take refuge in God. Psalm 34:8

What shall we return to God for all God's bounty to us?
We will lift the cup of salvation and call upon the name of God. We will pay our vows to God in the presence of all the people. Psalm 116:12-14

Christ, our paschal lamb, has been sacrificed. Therefore, let us celebrate the festival.
Not with the old yeast, the yeast of malice and evil, but with the unleavened bread of sincerity and truth.
1 Corinthians 5:7-8

Prayers of Remembrance and Thanksgiving

Almighty God, Giver of all mercies, we your unworthy servants do give you most humble and hearty thanks for all your goodness and loving-kindness to us and all people.

We bless you for our creation, preservation, and all the blessings of this life; but above all, for your inestimable love in the redemption of the world by our Lord Jesus Christ, for the means of grace, and for the hope of glory. And, we beseech you, give to us a due sense of all your mercies, that our hearts may be fully thankful; and that we may show forth your praise, not only with our lips but in our lives, by giving up ourselves to your service and by walking before you in holiness and righteousness all our days; through Jesus Christ our Lord, to whom, with you and the Holy Spirit, be all honor and glory, world without end. **Amen.** A General Thanksgiving

Almighty and most merciful God, from whom comes every good and perfect gift, we give you praise and hearty thanks for all your mercies. For your goodness that created us, your bounty that has sustained us, your parental discipline that has reprimanded and corrected us, your patience that has borne with us, and your love that has redeemed us, we praise you. For Christ our Savior, for your Spirit our comforter, for your church our home, for the lives of all godly men and women, and for the hope of life to come, we praise you, O God. Grant to us, with all your gifts, a heart to love and worship you; and enable us to show our thankfulness for your benefits by giving ourselves to your service and by conforming in all things to your will. **Amen.**[1]

Thanks be to you, Jesus Christ, for all the benefits you have given us, for the pains and insults which you have

---

[1]Reprinted from *The Book of Common Order of the Church of Scotland* by permission of Oxford University Press, adapted.

borne for us. Most merciful redeemer, friend, and brother, may we know you more clearly, love you more dearly, and follow you more nearly, now and ever. **Amen.**

Richard of Chichester, 1197–1233

Loving God, who has given us the ability to make and to break the bonds of friendship and affection with others, we give you thanks for those whose lives are intertwined with ours and who give so much of themselves to bring joy and security to us. Grant, O God, that we might have the spirit to make these relationships even more stable and to rebuild the indifferent or hostile relationships that divide us from others. Give us strength to follow your commandment to love everyone as you love them. **Amen.**

Creator God, we thank you for the beauty of the world around us: for flowers and trees, for streams and seas, for sunshine and rain, for fish and animals, but especially for women and men whose lives have made your world a richer and more beautiful place. May we, with them, devote ourselves to preserving your creation that those who follow after us may find the world a good and beautiful habitat in which to live. **Amen.**

Gracious God, who has come to us in Jesus Christ and who has revealed to us through his life and teachings the sense and purpose of our own lives, we give you sincere thanks that we have heard the liberating Word of the gospel. Grant that we may continue strong in the faith and be ever earnest to share with others the good news that in Christ all people can be free. **Amen.**

Lift up your hearts:
We lift them up to God.

Let us give thanks to our God:

It is fitting and right so to do.

What shall we render to God for all God's benefits toward us?

We shall offer to God the sacrifice of thanksgiving, for yours, O God, is the greatness and the power and the victory and the majesty forever!

For your perfect wisdom and perfect goodness, for the fullness of your love revealed to us through Jesus Christ our Savior:

With thanksgiving we worship and praise you, O God. Amen.

Give thanks to God, for God is good:

For God's steadfast love endures forever.

Let us pray:

For accepting us despite ourselves,

For your grace that continually renews hope in us and remakes our lives:

We thank you, God.

For your providence that sustains and supports us,

For your love that reproves and restores us:

We thank you, God.

For minds that make us restless until we know the truth:

We thank you, God.

For faith that promises triumph over doubt:

We thank you, God.

For fleeting glimpses of reality, for visions we cannot describe, for depths we can but feel:

We thank you, God, and give you praise now and forevermore. Amen.

God, merciful and gracious, hear our words of thanksgiving which we offer to you:

For the wonders of creation, for your wisdom inspiring the thoughts and works of men and women, for your love as seen in Jesus Christ:

Thanks be to you, O God.

For the delight of living, for home and friends, and for the joy of loving and being loved:

Thanks be to you, O God.

For the ardor to love you, for the privilege to pray to you, and for your answer to our petitions:

Thanks be to you, O God. Amen.

We offer thanks to you, gracious God, for your presence with humankind throughout the ages, revealing with increasing fullness your grace and truth; and for prophets, saints, benefactors, and all who have loved you and have revealed that love in word and deed:

We give you thanks.

Especially we offer thanks to you, gracious God, for Jesus Christ, the Word Incarnate, who brought life and liberty to all. For his life, his ministry, and his call to us and to all peoples everywhere to follow him:

We give you thanks. Amen.

Hear, O God, our prayers of thanksgiving for your abiding presence with us. *(Silent prayer)*

Hear, O God, our prayer of thanksgiving for your love revealed in Jesus Christ. *(Silent prayer)*

Hear, O God, our prayers of thanksgiving for your call to discipleship. *(Silent prayer)*

Hear, O God, our thankful response to your summons. *(Silent prayer)*

Accept our thanks, O God, and to you be glory, forever and ever, world without end. Amen.

Prayers of Thanksgiving at the Lord's Supper

Be present with us now, O Christ, as you were with your disciples in the upper room. Preside at your table, and give us of the bread of life, even yourself, that we may be nourished not only as we sit at table, but throughout the days and weeks ahead. To you we give our thanks. **Amen.**

Not as we ought, but as we are able, we offer thanks to you, O God, for Jesus Christ. We thank you for his life and ministry, for his sacrificial death on the cross, and for his resurrection and the promise he gives to all who believe in him that they too shall share in the new life in him.
To Christ be honor and glory, now and forever.
Through the eating of the bread and the drinking of the wine help us to remember Jesus Christ, his life and death, his words and work. Consecrate by your Spirit this bread and wine, that they may become the way to a vital encounter with the living Christ.
Accept our offering of praise and thanksgiving, and receive us as we dedicate ourselves anew to you. Amen.

As we are gathered about this table, let each of us offer thanks.
(Silence)
Gracious God, who has given us these elements of bread and wine as a living remembrance of our Savior, open our hearts and minds to receive this sacrament, and grant that in receiving it we may receive Christ as a living presence and be strengthened in our fellowship one with another to your glory, now and forever. **Amen.**
Let us give thanks to God our Creator and Redeemer.
Let us give thanks for our daily work, for the skills and

responsibilities we exercise and for the opportunity to labor together in home, office, school, factory, and in all places for the common good.

We give you thanks, our Creator and Redeemer.

Let us give thanks for loving companions, for family and friends, for fellow workers, for those who serve us in so many ways, and for each other.

We give you thanks, our Creator and Redeemer.

Let us give thanks for food and drink, for clothing and shelter, for those who provide health care, and all others who bring strength and comfort to us.

We give you thanks, our Creator and Redeemer.

Let us give thanks for the church throughout the world, and for this congregation.

We give you thanks, our Creator and Redeemer.

Let us give thanks for this sacred meal, for the fellowship we have with one with another, for the remembrance we have of Jesus Christ, and for the present blessing he has promised to us when we faithfully partake of the bread and wine.

We give you thanks, our Creator and Redeemer, to whom be glory now and forever. Amen.

Into the World

Ascriptions of Glory

Now to our God, who by the power at work within us is able to accomplish abundantly far more than all we can ask or imagine, to God be glory in the church and in Christ Jesus to all generations, forever and ever. **Amen.**

Ephesians 3:20-21

To the King of the ages, immortal, invisible, the only God, be honor and glory forever and ever. **Amen.**

1 Timothy 1:17

Now to the one who is able to keep you from falling, and to make you stand without blemish in the presence of divine glory with rejoicing, to the only God our Savior, through Jesus Christ our Lord, be glory, majesty, power, and authority, before all time and now and forever. **Amen.**   Jude 24

To Christ who loves us and freed us from our sins by his blood, and made us to be a kingdom of priests serving his God and Father, to him be glory and dominion forever and ever. **Amen.**

Revelation 1:5-6

Glory be to the Father, and to the Son, and to the Holy Spirit; as it was in the beginning, is now, and ever shall be, world without end. **Amen.**

To the King eternal, immortal, invisible, the only wise God, be honor and glory, praise and adoration, dominion and power, world without end. **Amen.**

Grace and peace to you from Jesus Christ. To him be glory and dominion forever and ever. **Amen.**

To the God of all grace, who has called us into eternal glory by Christ Jesus, be glory and dominion and power, forever and ever. **Amen.**

Blessings and Benedictions

God bless you and keep you.
God's face shine upon you and be gracious to you.
God look upon you with love and give you peace. **Amen.**

Numbers 6:24-26

God will keep your going out and coming in from this time on and forevermore. **Amen.** Psalm 121:8

May the God of steadfastness and encouragement grant you to live in harmony with one another, in accordance with Christ Jesus. **Amen.** Romans 15:5

The grace of Jesus Christ, the love of God, and the communion of the Holy Spirit be with all of you. **Amen.**
2 Corinthians 13:13

Now to our God, who by the power at work within us is able to accomplish abundantly far more than all we can ask or imagine, to God be glory in the church and in Christ Jesus to all generations, forever and ever. **Amen.**
Ephesians 3:20-21

The peace of God, which surpasses all understanding, will guard your hearts and your minds in Christ Jesus. **Amen.**
Philippians 4:7

Beloved, whatever is true, whatever is honorable, whatever is just, whatever is pure, whatever is pleasing, whatever is commendable, if there is any excellence and if there is anything worthy of praise, think about these things. Keep on doing the things that you have learned and received and heard and seen in me, and the God of peace will be with you. **Amen.** Philippians 4:8-9

May you be filled with the knowledge of God's will in all spiritual wisdom and understanding, so that you may lead lives worthy of God. **Amen.** Colossians 1:9-10

May you be made strong with all the strength that comes from God's glorious power, and may you be prepared to endure everything with patience, while joyfully giving thanks to God. **Amen.** Colossians 1:11-12

Now may the God of peace give you peace at all times in all ways, and the grace of our Lord Jesus Christ be with all of you. **Amen.** 2 Thessalonians 3:16,18

Now may the God of peace, who brought back from the dead our Lord Jesus, the great shepherd of the sheep, by the blood of the eternal covenant, make you complete in everything good so that you may do God's will, through Jesus Christ, to whom be the glory forever and ever. **Amen.** Hebrews 13:20-21

The God of all grace, who has called you to eternal glory in Christ, will restore, support, strengthen, and establish you. To God be the power forever and ever. **Amen.**
1 Peter 5:10-11

Grow in the grace and knowledge of our Lord and Savior Jesus Christ. To him be the glory both now and to the day of eternity. **Amen.** 2 Peter 3:18

Go in peace, and the blessing of God Almighty, Creator, Christ, and Holy Spirit, be upon you and remain with you always. **Amen.**

Go in peace; publish the gospel; visit the sick; comfort the dispirited; and may the love of God go with all of us. **Amen.**

Go in love, and may the grace, mercy, and peace of God abide in you. **Amen.**

Gracious God, who calls us both to worship and to work, our worship now is ended. Grant, we pray, that as we turn again to the tasks that lie before us, our work will not betray our worship, through Jesus Christ our Lord. **Amen.**

Go forth in peace, but not in complacency; be strong, but not arrogant; have conviction, but be understanding of the beliefs of others; be eager to love, but not meddlesome; be proud enough not to have contempt for yourselves, but sufficiently humble not to be jealous of your neighbors. Go forth in peace. **Amen.**

As you, O God, have blessed our coming in, now bless our going forth; and grant that when we leave your house we may not leave your presence, but be ever near us and keep us near to you. **Amen.**

Gracious God, at your table through the bread and the cup you have brought us once again to a remembrance of Jesus the Christ. Grant that as we leave this time of worship the memory of him may be to us a guiding light as we walk the path of our daily life. **Amen.** (*For use at the Lord's Supper*)

Go forth in joy. Love and serve one another. Be a faithful witness to God in the world and live in such a way that the gracious Spirit of Jesus may be with you in all that you do and say. **Amen.**

You have feasted at Christ's table. Your hunger has been satisfied and your thirst quenched. Go, therefore, and give drink to the thirsty and bread to the hungry, that they too may find life. **Amen.**

May the peace of God that passes all understanding fill your hearts and minds and bring you stability in the midst of an unstable world. Go in peace. **Amen.**

May God bless you with all good and keep you from all evil; may God give light to your hearts with loving wisdom and be gracious to you; may God's countenance be lifted up to you for eternal peace. **Amen.**

Dead Sea Scrolls, adapted

Gracious God, as we depart from this place of worship we pray that you will make us instruments of your peace; where there is hatred, let us sow love; where there is injury, pardon; where there is doubt, faith; where there is despair, hope; where there is darkness, light; and where there is sadness, comfort. **Amen.**

Francis of Assisi, 1182–1226; adapted

Loving God, as we go from worship into the world, grant that we may not so much seek to be consoled as to console; to be understood, as to understand; to be loved, as to love; for it is in giving that we receive, it is in pardoning that we are pardoned, and it is in dying that we are born to eternal life. **Amen.** Francis of Assisi, 1182–1226; adapted

May Christ be near you to defend you, within you to refresh you, around you to preserve you, before you to guide you, behind you to justify you, above you to bless you. **Amen.** Latin Prayer, tenth century

May the love of God which is broader than the measure of our minds, the grace of Lord Jesus Christ which is sufficient for all our needs, and the communion with the Holy Spirit which shall lead us into all truth, go with us this day and all our days. **Amen.** Esther Hargis, 1947–

Holy God, let your servants depart in peace; your word has been fulfilled. We have seen the salvation which you have prepared for all people as a light to reveal you to the nations. Go in peace. **Amen.** *Nunc Dimittis*, adapted

Versicles and Responses

Christ be with you. (Traditional: The Lord be with you.)
And with your spirit.

The peace of Christ be with you.
And also with you.
Lift up your hearts.
We lift them up to Christ. (Traditional: **We lift them up to the Lord.**)
Let us give thanks to God Most High.
It is right to give God thanks and praise.

Praise God, to whom all praise is due.
Praised be God whose glorious name is forever and forever.

Lord, have mercy upon us.   *Kyrie eleison.*
Christ, have mercy upon us.   *or*   ***Christe eleison.***
Lord, have mercy upon us.   *Kyrie eleison.*

O God, let your mercy be upon us;
As we put our trust in you.

O God, hear our prayer:
And let our cry come to you.
Let us pray.

Alleluia, Christ is risen.
Christ (or The Lord) is risen indeed.

Glory to God the Creator,
and to Christ,
and to the Holy Spirit:

as it was in the beginning, is now,
and will be forever. **Amen.** *Gloria*, adapted

Jesus, Lamb of God: have mercy on us.
Jesus, bearer of our sins: have mercy on us.
Jesus, redeemer of the world: give us peace.

Agnus Dei, adapted

The Lord's Prayer

Our Father who art in heaven,
Hallowed be thy name.
Thy kingdom come,
Thy will be done,
    On earth, as it is in heaven.
Give us this day our daily bread;
And forgive us our debts,
    As we also have forgiven our debtors;
And lead us not into temptation,
    But deliver us from evil.
For thine is the kingdom, and the power,
        and the glory, forever. **Amen.**
                    Revised Standard Version

Our Father, who art in heaven,
    hallowed be thy name.
    thy kingdom come,
    thy will be done,
    on earth, as it is in heaven.
Give us this day our daily bread.
And forgive us our trespasses,
    as we forgive those who trespass against us.
And lead us not into temptation,

but deliver us from evil.
For thine is the kingdom, and the power,
  and the glory, for ever and ever. **Amen.**

  Book of Common Prayer

Our Father in heaven,
  hallowed be your name.
Your kingdom come.
Your will be done,
  on earth as it is in heaven.
Give us this day our daily bread.
And forgive us our debts,
  as we also have forgiven our debtors.
And do not bring us to the time of trial,
  but rescue us from the evil one.
For the kingdom and the power and the
  glory are yours forever. **Amen.**

  New Revised Standard Version

Doxologies

Praise God, from whom all blessings flow;
Praise Christ, all people here below;
Praise Holy Spirit evermore;
Praise Triune God, whom we adore. **Amen.**

Praise God, from whom all blessings flow;
Praise God, all creatures here below;
Praise God above, you heavenly host;
Creator, Christ, and Holy Ghost. **Amen.**

To God Creator, God the Son,
And Holy Spirit, three in one,
Unceasing praise and glory be,
Now and through all eternity. **Amen.**

Part 3

Sentences and Prayers
for the Christian Year

The Christian year, beginning with the first Sunday in Advent, celebrates the events of the gospel. Through the seasons of Advent, Christmas, Epiphany, Lent, Holy Week, Easter, Ascension, and Pentecost the story of God's acts in Christ, the coming of the Holy Spirit, and the establishment of the church are told. In the remainder of the Christian year, during Kingdomtide or Trinity season, the church looks particularly at God's mission to the world.

A collection of sentences and prayers for these seasons of the Christian year are given. These by no means exhaust the richness of material that can be provided for each season. But when they are combined with the use of the lectionary, they will give to the congregation an orderly presentation of God's acts in history and a recurring reminder of the Creator's love for the world.

Advent

Advent begins the Christian year and marks the season of preparation for the coming of Christ, both in his incarnation and in his coming at the end of time. It is a season for reflection and anticipation, rich in meaning and in symbolism.

Sentences

Let the heavens be glad, and let the earth rejoice before the Lord, for God is coming to judge the earth. God will judge the world with righteousness, and the peoples with truth.

Psalm 96:11,13

Therefore God will give you a sign. Look, the young woman is with child and shall bear a son, and shall name him Immanuel.

Isaiah 7:14

The wilderness and the dry land shall be glad, the desert shall rejoice and blossom; and the ransomed of the Lord shall return, and come to Zion with singing; everlasting joy shall be upon their heads; they shall obtain joy and gladness, and sorrow and sighing shall flee away.

Isaiah 35:1-2,10

Comfort, O comfort my people, says your God. Speak tenderly to Jerusalem, and cry to her that she has served her term, that her penalty is paid, that she has received from God's hand double for all her sins.

Isaiah 40:1-2

The spirit of God is upon me and has anointed me; God has sent me to bring good news to the oppressed, to bind up the brokenhearted, to proclaim liberty to the captives, and release to the prisoners; to proclaim the year of God's favor.

Isaiah 61:1-2

For thus says the Lord of hosts: Once again, in a little while, I will shake the heavens and the earth and the sea and the dry land; and I will shake all the nations, so that the treasure of all nations shall come, and I will fill this house with splendor, says the Lord of hosts.

Haggai 2:6-7

Sing and rejoice, O daughter of Zion! For lo, I will come and dwell in your midst, says God. Many nations shall join themselves to me on that day, and you shall be my people, and I will dwell in your midst.   Zechariah 2:10-11

I am sending my messenger to prepare the way before me, and God whom you seek will suddenly come to the temple. The messenger of the covenant in whom you delight—indeed, he is coming, says the Lord of hosts.   Malachi 3:1

Behold, a virgin shall conceive and bear a son, and his name shall be called Emmanuel, which means, God with us.   Matthew 1:23 (RSV)

See, I am sending my messenger ahead of you, who will prepare your way; the voice of one crying out in the wilderness: "Prepare the way of the Lord, make God's paths straight."   Mark 1:2-3

By the tender mercy of our God, the dawn from on high will break upon us, to give light to those who sit in darkness and in the shadow of death, to guide our feet into the way of peace.   Luke 1:78-79

It is now the moment for you to wake from sleep. The night is far gone, the day is near. Let us then lay aside the works of darkness and put on the armor of light.   Romans 13:11-12

Surely God's salvation is at hand for those who fear the Lord, for God will speak peace to the people, to the faithful, to those who turn to God in their hearts.
   Surely God's salvation is at hand for those who fear the Lord, that God's glory may dwell in our land.
Steadfast love and faithfulness will meet; righteousness and peace will kiss each other.

**Faithfulness will spring up from the ground, and
righteousness will look down from the sky.**

God will give what is good, and our land will yield its
increase.

**Righteousness will go before, and will make a path
for God's steps.** Psalm 85:8-13

A shoot shall come out from the stump of Jesse, and a
branch shall grow out of the roots.

**The spirit of God shall rest on him, the spirit of wis-
dom and understanding, the spirit of counsel and
might, the spirit of knowledge and the fear of
God.** Isaiah 11:1-2

A voice cries out: "In the wilderness prepare the way of the
Lord, make straight in the desert a highway for our God.

**Every valley shall be lifted up, and every mountain
and hill be made low.**

The uneven ground shall become level, and the rough
places a plain.

**Then the glory of God shall be revealed, and all peo-
ple shall see it together, for the mouth of God has
spoken."** Isaiah 40:3-5

The days are surely coming, says God, when I will fulfill
the promise I made to the house of Israel and the house of
Judah.

**In those days and at that time God will cause a righ-
teous Branch to spring up for David; and he shall
execute justice and righteousness in the land.**

In those days Judah will be saved and Jerusalem will live
in safety.

**And this is the name by which it shall be called:
"God is our righteousness."** Jeremiah 33:14-16

My soul magnifies the Lord, and my spirit rejoices in God my Savior,

For God has looked with favor on the lowliness of God's servant.

Surely, from now on all generations will call me blessed; for the Mighty One has done great things for me, and holy is God's name.

God's mercy is on those who fear God, from generation to generation.

God has showed strength of arm and has scattered the proud in the thoughts of their hearts.

God has brought down the powerful from their thrones, and lifted up the lowly.

God has filled the hungry with good things, and sent the rich away empty.

God has helped the servant Israel, in remembrance of God's mercy,

According to the promise God made to our ancestors, to Abraham and to his descendants forever.

The Magnificat of Mary, Luke 1:47-55

Prayers

Our heavenly Creator, our spirits turn at this season not only to the coming of your Son into history in the form of a baby, but also to your coming in Spirit. We ask you, O God, to pour out your Spirit upon all who walk in darkness. Grant your power to the weak; your love to those who hate; and your peace to those who know only the ugliness of strife, struggle, and turmoil. If it be your will, make us instruments of your power, love, and peace for those who do not know you. Hear now our prayer. **Amen.**

Send us into the world in your name, God. In this season, grant us your power, that our weakness may become strength. Grant us your love, that any hatred may be overcome. And pour forth your peace, that our anxieties may find comfort in you; through Jesus Christ. **Amen.**

You, O God, come to us in our deepest moment of need. You always come to the one who calls upon you. You who spoke of old through the prophets, make plain to us their message, that we may come to know it in our day. For your grace, that we might have open hearts to receive him whose coming we celebrate in this season, we humbly pray, O God. **Amen.**

Let us receive the light and we will receive God. Let us receive the light and become disciples of the Lord. Sing, O Word; reveal the Creator to us. Your words will save us and your songs will teach us. We are the people of God's love. Let us sing, and never cease, to the God of peace above. **Amen.**   Clement of Alexandria, adapted

Surely God is our salvation; we will trust, and will not be afraid,
>   **For God is our strength and our might; God has become our salvation.**

With joy we will draw water from the wells of salvation, and we will say in that day:
>   **Give thanks and call on God's name; make known God's deeds among the nations. Amen.**   Isaiah 12:2-4

Blessed are you, eternal God:
>   **In whom the heavens rejoice and the earth is glad, for you will judge the world in righteousness.**

Blessed are you, Christ our Savior:
Who will come in power and great glory to perfect your kingdom, and to bring in God's ransomed with songs of everlasting joy.
Blessed are you, holy and gracious Spirit:
Who quickens our hearts and fills our mouths with praise. Glory be to you, O God, forever and ever. Amen.

God, whose Word took flesh and came to dwell among us,
We lift our hearts to you.
May we open our ears to your voice,
And hear the good news: a Savior is coming!
The long-promised One is coming; let us prepare.
Let us open our hearts to receive the Spirit. Amen.

Hark the glad sound! The Savior comes,
The Savior promised long;
Let every heart prepare a throne
And every voice a song.
**Our glad hosannas, Prince of Peace,
Your welcome shall proclaim,
And heaven's eternal arches ring
With your beloved name. Amen.**

Philip Doddridge, 1702–1751

Christmas

The Christmas season consists of twelve days, beginning with the festival of the Nativity. This time of celebration centers upon the birth of Jesus, the good news that was proclaimed by the heavenly host to all people.

Sentences

Do not be afraid; for see—I am bringing you good news of great joy for all the people: to you is born this day in the city of David a Savior, who is the Messiah, the Lord.

Luke 2:10-11

Glory to God in the highest heaven, and on earth peace among those whom God favors. Luke 2:14

Lord, you now let your servants go in peace, according to your word; for our eyes have seen your salvation, which you have prepared in the sight of all peoples, a light to reveal you to all nations, and for glory to your people Israel. Luke 2:29-32, adapted

The Word became flesh and lived among us, full of grace and truth. John 1:14

Long ago God spoke to our ancestors in many and various ways by the prophets, but in these last days God has spoken to us by a Son. Hebrews 1:1-2

O sing to the Lord a new song, for God has done marvelous things.
God's right hand and holy arm have gotten the victory.
God has remembered steadfast love and faithfulness to the house of Israel.
All the ends of the earth have seen the victory of our God.
Make a joyful noise to God, all the earth;
Break forth into joyous song and sing praises.

Psalm 98:1,3-4

The people who walked in darkness have seen a great light; those who lived in a land of deep darkness—on them light has shined.

For a child has been born for us, a son given to us; authority rests upon his shoulders; and he is named Wonderful Counselor, Mighty God, Everlasting Father, Prince of Peace. Isaiah 9:2,6

Blessed be the God of Israel, who has looked favorably on the people and redeemed them.

God has raised up a mighty savior for us in the house of God's servant David.

God spoke through the mouth of the holy prophets from of old, that we would be saved from our enemies and from the hand of all who hate us.

Thus God has shown the mercy promised to our ancestors, remembering God's holy covenant.

And the child will be called the prophet of the Most High, the One who will go before, to prepare God's ways,

To give knowledge of salvation to God's people by the forgiveness of their sins.

By the tender mercy of our God, the dawn from on high will break upon us, to give light to those who sit in darkness and in the shadow of death,

To guide our feet into the way of peace.

Luke 1:68-72,76-79

Prayers

Almighty God, you made this holy night shine with the brightness of the true light. Grant that here on earth we may walk in the light of Christ's presence and in the last day wake to the brightness of his glory; through Jesus Christ our Lord. **Amen.**[1]

You came to us in humility as a baby, O God. Now grow in our hearts, that with your peace and grace we might go forth into the world determined in our faith to meet the issues of life with courage and humility. **Amen.**

You have wonderfully created us, O God, and yet more wonderfully restored the dignity of human nature. Grant that we may share the divine life of him who humbled himself to share our humanity, your Son Jesus Christ. **Amen.**   Book of Common Prayer, adapted

Our holy God, who presented humankind with the great and glorious gift of your Son Jesus Christ, we humbly bow and present our small gifts and with them our lives. Do not count this offering for its actual worth, but take what we give and who we are for your service; through Jesus Christ. **Amen.**

Almighty and everlasting God, who sent Christ into the world not just for us but for all the world, we ask you to hear the prayers of your servants as we lift up our hearts in intercession for the world.
Let us pray for the child who has no welcome room in the world.
(Silence)

---

[1]Reprinted by permission from the Dec. 24, 1991 CELEBRATE worship supplement, copyright © Augsburg Fortress.

Let us pray for those in the world who suffer from hunger and who are homeless.
(Silence)
Let us pray for those in the world who suffer from injustice.
(Silence)
You have heard the prayers of your people, O God. We who are your servants and the servants of our brothers and sisters do humbly ask your power and love, so we may guide others in unity, through Jesus Christ. **Amen.**

Christ is born, give glory! Christ comes from heaven, meet him! Christ is on earth, be exalted!
   O all the earth, sing unto God, and sing praises in gladness, all you people, for God has been glorified.
Wisdom and Word and Power, Christ is the Son and the brightness of God; Christ was made human, and so has won us to God.
   O all the earth, sing unto God, and sing praises in gladness, all you people, for God has been glorified. Amen.   Eastern Orthodox prayer

Lift up your hearts:
   We lift them up to God.
Let us give thanks to our God:
   It is right and good to do so.
We praise you, God, for all the joy of this season. We sing gladly our hymns and carols. We give our gifts to one another in joy. But above all we thank you for the matchless gift of our Savior, Jesus Christ.
   Give us lives that will in their deeds fully praise you. Give us love, that we may love him who has loved us and who gave himself for us, Christ our Lord. Amen.

Our hearts for very joy doth leap
Our lips no more their silence keep;
We too must sing with joyful tongue
That sweetest ancient cradle-song:
Glory to God in highest heaven,
Who unto us a Son has given;
While angels sing with holy mirth
A glad new year to all the earth. Amen.

Martin Luther, 1483–1546; adapted

Epiphany

The season of Epiphany celebrates the manifestation of God's light and power in Christ, beginning with the visit of the star-led Magi to the child Jesus and continuing through the stories of his baptism and early miracles to the church's mission to the Gentiles.

Sentences

The wise ones set out; and there, ahead of them went the star that they had seen at its rising, until it stopped over the place where the child was. On entering the house, they saw the child with Mary his mother; and they knelt down and worshiped him. Matthew 2:9,11

Lord, now you are dismissing your servant in peace, according to your word; for my eyes have seen your salvation, which you have prepared in the presence of all peoples, a light for revelation to the Gentiles and for glory to your people Israel. Luke 2:29-32

Jesus said: "I am the light of the world. Whoever follows me will never walk in darkness but will have the light of life."   John 8:12

Those who fear God rise in the darkness as a light for the upright;
They are gracious, merciful, and righteous.
It is well with those who deal generously and lend, who conduct their affairs with justice.
For the righteous will never be moved; they will be remembered forever.
They are not afraid of evil tidings; their hearts are firm, secure in God.
Their hearts are steady, they will not be afraid.
                                                    Psalm 112:4-8

Arise, shine; for your light has come, and the glory of God has risen upon you.
For darkness shall cover the earth, and thick darkness the peoples;
But God will arise upon you, and God's glory will appear over you.
Nations shall come to your light, and kings to the brightness of your dawn.   Isaiah 60:1-3

In the beginning was the Word, and the Word was with God, and the Word was God.
All things came into being through God, and without God not one thing came into being.
What has come into being was life, and the life was the light of all people.
The light shines in the darkness and the darkness did not overcome it.   John 1:1-5

Prayers

You wonderfully created and yet more wonderfully restored the dignity of human nature, O God. In your mercy, let us share the divine life of Jesus Christ who came to share our humanity, and who lives with you and the Holy Spirit, now and forever. **Amen.**[2]

O Splendor of God's glory bright,
From Light eternal bringing light,
O Light of life, the living Spring,
True Day, all days illumining.
> **Dawn's glory gilds the earth and skies;**
> **Let him, our perfect Morn, arise,**
> **The Word in God Almighty one,**
> **Creator imaged in the Son. Amen.**

> > Ambrose of Milan, c.339–397; adapted

As the wise ones of old came bearing gifts, so we come to you, God, with our gifts. Accept and transform them in the light of the gospel, that the world might believe and come to know him whom to know is life eternal, Christ Jesus, our Lord. **Amen.**

Holy are you, O God, our light and our salvation, and blessed is Jesus Christ, in whom you have revealed yourself. You sent a star to guide wise ones to where the Christ was born; and your signs and witnesses in every age have led your people from far places to his light. For Jesus Christ, we thank you. **Amen.**

---

[2]Reprinted by permission from the Dec. 29, 1991 CELEBRATE worship supplement, copyright © Augsburg Fortress.

Jesus, in his baptism and in table fellowship, took his place with sinners. Your Spirit anointed him to preach good news to the poor,

To proclaim release to the captives and recovering of sight to the blind,

To set at liberty those who are oppressed, and to announce that the time had come when you would save your people.

By your Holy Spirit make us one with Christ, one with each other, and one in ministry to all the world, until Christ comes in final victory and we feast at his heavenly banquet. Amen.[3]

From the rising of the sun to its setting, let the name of God be praised.

You are our lamp. You, O God, make our darkness bright.

Light and peace in Jesus Christ our Lord.

Thanks be to God. Amen.

To you, God, who brought kings to seek and adore the Christ child, we pray that you would lead your church into all the dark places of the earth, bearing the torch of Christ's light, so that the day may soon come when all men and women on earth shall honor the ruler of all, Jesus Christ our Lord.

O God, hear the prayer of your people.

God, who led the kings of the East to bow the knee before the majesty of the infant Jesus, in order that all may come to know and learn the ways of the Prince of Peace, Jesus Christ our Lord.

_____

[3]Reprinted by permission from the Jan. 26, 1992 CELEBRATE worship supplement, copyright © Augsburg Fortress.

O God, hear the prayer of your people.
We ask, God, that you guide all those who are laboring for
the spread of your gospel among the nations, that the
whole world may be filled with the knowledge of your
truth.

**O God, hear the prayer of your people, through
Jesus Christ your Son. Amen.**

Lent

Lent is a forty-day period of spiritual discipline and reflection,
beginning with Ash Wednesday. It is a season for growth
through repentance, and a preparation for sharing in the passion
of Jesus Christ.

Sentences

God is merciful and gracious, slow to anger and abounding in steadfast love. If we confess our sins, God who is
faithful and just will forgive us our sins and cleanse us
from all unrighteousness.   Psalm 103:8; 1 John 1:9

For God, the Holy One of Israel, has said, ''In returning
and rest you shall be saved; in quietness and in trust shall
be your strength.''   Isaiah 30:15

Then your light shall break forth like the dawn, and your
healing shall spring up quickly; your vindicator shall go
before you, the glory of God shall be your rear guard.
Then you shall call, and be answered; you shall cry for
help, and God will say, Here I am.   Isaiah 58:8-9

Rend your hearts and not your clothing. Return to the Lord
your God, who is gracious and merciful, slow to anger,
and abounding in steadfast love.   Joel 2:13

Then Jesus said: "If any want to become my followers, let them deny themselves and take up their cross and follow me."   Matthew 16:24

The apostles gathered around Jesus, and he said to them, "Come away to a deserted place all by yourselves and rest a while."   Mark 6:30-31

I will get up and go to my father, and I will say to him, "Father, I have sinned against heaven and before you; I am no longer worthy to be called your child." Luke 15:18

Hear the words of our Lord Jesus: "I am the good shepherd. The good shepherd lays down his life for the sheep."
                                                        John 10:11

God's love is proved for us in that while we still were sinners Christ died for us.   Romans 5:8

Do you not know that all of us who have been baptized into Christ Jesus were baptized into his death? Therefore we have been buried with him by baptism into death, so that, just as Christ was raised from the dead by the glory of God, so we too might walk in newness of life.
                                                        Romans 6:3-4

Draw near to God, and God will draw near to you. Humble yourselves before God, and you will be exalted.
                                                        James 4:8,10

For to this you have been called, because Christ also suffered for you, leaving you an example, that you should follow in his steps.   1 Peter 2:21

In this is love, not that we loved God but that God loved us and sent Jesus Christ to be the atoning sacrifice for our sins. Beloved, since God loved us so much, we also ought to love one another. 1 John 4:10-11

To you, O God, we lift up our souls. In you, O God, we trust; do not let us be put to shame; do not let our enemies exult over us.

Make us to know your ways, O God, teach us your paths, and lead us in your truth.

For you are the God of our salvation; for you we wait all day long.

Be mindful of your mercy, O God, and of your steadfast love, for they have been from of old.

Do not remember the sins of our youth or our transgressions.

According to your steadfast love remember us, for your goodness' sake, O God! Psalm 25:1-2,4-7

Out of the depths we cry to you. God, hear our voice!

Let your ears be attentive to the voice of our supplications.

If you, O God, should mark iniquities, who could stand? But there is forgiveness with you, so that you may be revered.

We wait for God, our souls wait and in God's word we hope.

Our souls wait for God more than those who watch for the morning.

O Israel, hope in God!

For with God there is steadfast love, and with God is great power to redeem.

It is God who will redeem Israel from all its iniquities. Psalm 130

We know that all things work together for good for those who love God, who are called according to God's purpose. What then are we to say?

If God is for us, who is against us?

God, who did not withhold God's own Son but gave him up for all of us, will God not with him also give us everything else?

Who will separate us from the love of Christ?

Will hardship, or distress, or persecution, or famine, or nakedness, or peril, or sword?

No, in all these things we are more than conquerors through the one who loved us.

For neither death, nor life, nor angels, nor rulers, nor things present, nor things to come,

Nor powers, nor height, nor depth, nor anything else in all creation, will be able to separate us from the love of God in Christ Jesus.

Romans 8:28,31-32,35,37-39

God, who is rich in mercy, out of great love to us even when we were dead through our trespasses, made us alive together with Christ.

By grace we have been saved.

We have been raised up with Christ and seated in heavenly places with him, so that in the ages to come we might know the immeasurable riches of God's grace.

By grace we have been saved.

For by grace we have been saved through faith, and this is not our own doing; it is the gift of God.

For we are what God has made us, created in Christ Jesus to do good as our way of life. Ephesians 2:4-10

If we say we have no sin, we deceive ourselves, and the truth is not in us.

If we confess our sins, God is faithful and just to forgive us our sins and cleanse us from all unrighteousness. 1 John 1:8-9

Prayers

You who led your ancient people through the wilderness and brought them to the promised land, guide now the people of this congregation, that, following our Savior, we may walk through the wilderness of this world toward the glory of the world to come; through Jesus Christ. **Amen.**[4]

In complete faithfulness you stand, O God, outside the door of our hearts, knocking again and again. Give us the will to open our lives to you. Make your home within our hearts, that we may love even as you have loved us; through Jesus Christ, our Lord. **Amen.**

We do not understand our own actions; we do the very things we know are wrong. God, we believe; help our unbelief! **Amen.**

We know that we have been made for your glory, God; yet we hide from you and have tried to escape your presence. Forgive us and bring us once again to the place where we may see you and sing praises to your majesty; through Jesus Christ. **Amen.**

Eternal God, your kingdom has broken into our troubled world through the life, death, and resurrection of your Son.

---

[4]Reprinted by permission from the Mar. 8, 1992 CELEBRATE worship supplement, copyright © Augsburg Fortress.

Help us to hear your Word and obey it, so that we may become instruments of your redeeming love; through your Son, Jesus Christ. **Amen.**[5]

Jesus Christ, who for our sake fasted forty days and forty nights, we ask for grace to discipline ourselves during this season, so that our bodies, minds, and spirits may become fitting vessels of your grace. Lead us into the paths of righteousness for your name's sake. **Amen.**

Almighty God, you know we are tempted to give up our disciplines of faithfulness, to focus on worldly pleasures instead of being rooted in your truth. Give us strength to return steadfastly to the way of discipleship; through Jesus Christ, your Son. **Amen.**

O God, you showed your love for humankind in the gift of Jesus Christ and brought him to our remembrance through your Spirit. We raise our voices in praise to you for his days upon the earth, his victory over temptation, his acts of love and mercy, his simple teaching concerning your way, his faithfulness even to death, and his victory in the cross and resurrection. Thanks be to you, O God, for your unspeakable gift in Jesus Christ. **Amen.**

Have mercy on us, O God, according to your steadfast love; according to your abundant mercy blot out our transgressions.
>   **Wash us thoroughly from our iniquities and cleanse us from our sins.**

---

[5]Reprinted by permission from the Mar. 22, 1992 CELEBRATE worship supplement, copyright © Augsburg Fortress.

Create in us clean hearts, O God, and put a new and right spirit within us.

Do not cast us away from your presence, and do not take your Holy Spirit from us.

Restore to us the joy of your salvation and sustain in us a willing spirit.

Open our lips, O God, and our mouths will declare your praise. Amen.   Psalm 51:1-2,10-12,15

Loving God, you have always been our help.

We cry to you and you hear us.

You bring healing to your people and deliver us from death.

You have turned our grief to dancing and our sorrow to joy.

Our hearts sing to you, gracious God; we will praise you forever. **Amen.**

God in heaven, the love of Jesus led him to accept the suffering of the cross that his sisters and brothers might glory in new life.

Change our selfishness, O God, into self-giving.

Help us to embrace the world you have given us, that the darkness of its pain may be transformed into the life and joy of Easter.

Grant this, we pray, through Jesus Christ. Amen.[6]

Lord Jesus, our Savior, let us now come to you:

Our hearts are cold; Lord, warm them with your selfless love.

---

[6]Reprinted by permission from the Apr. 5, 1992 CELEBRATE worship supplement, copyright © Augsburg Fortress.

Our hearts are sinful; cleanse them with your precious blood.

Our hearts are weak; strengthen them with your joyous Spirit.

Our hearts are empty; fill them with your divine presence.

Lord Jesus, our hearts are yours; possess them always and only for yourself. Amen.

Augustine of Hippo

Jesus walked that lonesome valley,
He had to walk it by himself;
O, nobody else could walk it for him,
He had to walk it by himself.

Help us, O God, to walk our lonesome valleys, knowing that we are not forsaken, for you are always walking beside us. Amen.

Traditional African American spiritual

Palm Sunday

Sentences

The stone that the builders rejected has become the cornerstone; this was God's doing, and it is amazing in our eyes.

Matthew 21:42

Hosanna to the Son of David! Blessed is the one who comes in the name of God! Hosanna in the highest heaven! Say to daughter Zion, "See, your salvation comes; his reward is with him, and his recompense before him." Blessed be the one who comes in the name of God!

Matthew 21:9; Isaiah 62:11

When the days drew near for him to be taken up, he set his face to go to Jerusalem.

Luke 9:51

The crowds that went ahead of him and that followed were shouting, "Hosanna to the Son of David! Blessed is the one who comes in the name of God! Hosanna in the highest heaven!"   Matthew 21:9

Blessed is the one who comes in the name of God:
Hosanna in the highest.
Lift up your heads, O gates! and be lifted up, O ancient doors!
That the King of glory may come in!
Who is this King of glory?
The Lord of hosts is the King of glory!
                                                    Matthew 21:9; Psalm 24:9-10

Prayers

On this day we keep the special memory of our Redeemer's entry into the city of Jerusalem: now and always may he triumph in our hearts. Let the God of grace and glory enter in, and let us offer ourselves and all we are in full and joyful tribute; through Jesus Christ. **Amen.**

Merciful God, your son Jesus steadfastly walked the road to Jerusalem, knowing that a cross stood at the journey's end. Grant us courage, that we, like Jesus, might walk toward the cross, strengthened by the one who is our Redeemer. **Amen.**

Sovereign God, brighten our spirits and open our mouths so that we may sing your praises throughout this day of joy.
All who know of your healing power shout, "Hosanna!"

All who know of your passion for justice shout, "Hosanna!"

All who know of your patient mercy shout, "Hosanna!"

All who know of your wondrous love shout, "Hosanna!"

Let everything that breathes shout, "Hosanna!"

Let even the stones shout, "Hosanna!"

Blessed be the One who comes in the name of the Lord! Amen!   Roger Balcom, 1959–

O merciful God, on this Palm Sunday we rejoice that you love us still, with a love that neither ebbs nor flows, a love that does not grow weary but is constant, year after year, age after age. Let our prayers of intercession be as palm branches before you.

We pray for all those who give their lives in service and sacrifice in their devotion to you.

We pray for all who face great temptation,

All who stagger under burdens too great for them to bear, all who live in surroundings that breed ignorance and evil.

We pray for people around the world.

We pray for refugees everywhere.

We pray for those in our own faith community.

(Silence)

In intercession we offer ourselves to you through our actions as well as our prayers: we ask that all who come to you in prayer may be filled with your grace. **Amen.**

Teach us, O God, that unless we walk through the darkness we cannot appreciate the light;

That unless we see the cross clearly, we will not understand the empty tomb;

That unless we obey even to the point of sacrifice, we cannot truly be your disciples.

In Christ's name we pray. Amen.

Maundy Thursday

This day of Holy Week derives its title from the Latin *mandatum novum*, the "new commandment" Jesus gave in John 13:34. Maundy Thursday worship services focus upon Christ's last passover meal with his disciples, through the sharing of bread and cup "in remembrance." Some churches as part of their Maundy Thursday worship follow the example of Jesus with an act of footwashing.

Sentences

Whoever wishes to be great among you must be your servant, and whoever wishes to be first among you must be your slave; just as the Christ came not to be served but to serve, and to give his life as a ransom for many.

Matthew 20:26-28

While they were eating, Jesus took a loaf of bread, and after blessing it he broke it, gave it to the disciples, and said, "Take, eat; this is my body." Then he took a cup, and after giving thanks he gave it to them, saying, "Drink from it, all of you; for this is my blood of the covenant, which is poured out for many for the forgiveness of sins."

Matthew 26:26-28

When the hour came, Jesus took his place at the table, and the apostles with him. He said to them, "I have eagerly desired to eat this Passover with you before I suffer; for I tell you, I will not eat it until it is fulfilled in the kingdom of God."   Luke 22:14-16

Jesus rose from supper, laid aside his garments, and girded himself with a towel. Then he poured water into a basin, and began to wash the disciples' feet, and to wipe them with the towel. He came to Simon Peter; and Peter said to him, "Lord, do you wash my feet?" Jesus answered him, "What I am doing you do not know now, but afterward you will understand." Peter said to him, "You shall never wash my feet." Jesus answered him, "If I do not wash you, you have no part in me." Peter said to him, "Lord, not my feet only but also my hands and my head!"

John 13:4-10 (RSV)

We love God, because our voices and our supplications have been heard.

God inclined an ear to us, therefore we will call on God as long as we live.

What shall we return to God for all these blessings given?

We will lift up the cup of salvation and call on God's name.

We will pay our vows to God, in the presence of the faithful, in the courts of God's house.

We are your servants, O God.   Psalm 116:1-2,12-19

Prayers

Help us, O God, to take towel and basin and in humbleness of spirit to wash the feet of those in need; through Jesus Christ, who came and who served. **Amen.**

O Lord, as this wine was once many grapes, and as this bread was once scattered in the fields, and as both are here gathered into one: so gather your church from every city and suburb, village and house, and make of us one living, holy church to serve you and to carry out your will. **Amen.**[7]

Help us, O God, to humble ourselves as did your Son Jesus Christ, who was beaten, spat upon, and crucified, and who died that your boundless love might be made known. **Amen.**

O God, we are thankful for the example of Christ, who before his passion prayed for his disciples and all who would believe through their word. We would join him in intercession for our brothers and sisters. We especially commend to your care all who face great temptation, all who stagger under burdens too heavy for them to bear, all whose spirits are broken, all who live in an environment of ignorance and evil. Open to them your ways and help us to walk with them, sharing their burdens; through Jesus Christ, who bore the cross. **Amen.**

Almighty and merciful God, the fountain of all goodness, who knows the thoughts of our hearts:
  We confess that we have sinned against you.
Wash us, we implore you, from the stains of our past sins.
  Give us grace and power to put away all offenses,
Being delivered from the bondage of sin, may we bring forth fruits worthy of repentance, and at last enter into your promised joy;
  Through the mercy of your blessed One, Jesus Christ. Amen.   Alcuin, c.732–804; adapted

---

[7]Reprinted by permission from the Mar. 15, 1992 CELEBRATE worship supplement, copyright © Augsburg Fortress.

Sentences and Prayers for the Christian Year

The love of Christ has gathered us as one.
Let us rejoice and be glad in him.
Let us fear and love the living God
And in purity of heart let us love one another.
  Where charity and love are, there is God.
When therefore we are gathered together
Let us not be divided in spirit.
Let bitter strife and discord cease between us;
Let Christ our God be present in our midst.
  Where charity and love are, there is God.
With all the blessed may we see for ever
Your face in glory, Jesus Christ our God.
Joy that is infinite and undefiled
For all the ages of eternity.
  Where charity and love are, there is God. Amen.

Western Rite

Good Friday

Sentences

He was despised and rejected by others; a man of suffering and acquainted with grief.   Isaiah 53:3

He was wounded for our transgressions, crushed for our iniquities; upon him was the punishment that made us whole, and by his bruises we are healed.   Isaiah 53:5

Is it nothing to you, all you who pass by? Look and see if there is any sorrow like my sorrow.   Lamentations 1:12

If any want to become my followers, let them deny themselves and take up their cross and follow me. For those who want to save their life will lose it; and those who lose their life for my sake will find it.   Matthew 16:24-25

Christ Jesus emptied himself, taking the form of a servant, being born in human likeness. And being found in human form, he humbled himself and became obedient to the point of death—even death on a cross.   Philippians 2:7-8

Prayers

God our Creator, we give thanks that your Word, Jesus Christ, spoke peace to a sinful world and brought reconciliation by the suffering and death he endured. Teach us, the people who bear his name, to follow the example he gave us. May our faith, hope, and charity turn hatred to love, conflict to peace. May his death and resurrection turn our death to eternal life. We ask this through Christ Jesus. **Amen.**[8]

Almighty God, even as Christ entered not into glory before he was crucified, mercifully grant that we, walking in the way of the cross, may find it the way of life and peace; through Jesus Christ. **Amen**.

Thanks be to you, O God, for Jesus Christ, who for the joy that was set before him endured the cross.
Thanks be to you, O God, for Jesus Christ, who in the cross triumphed over sin and death, principalities and powers and over all who would seek to deny you.

---

[8]Reprinted by permission from the Mar. 29, 1992 CELEBRATE worship supplement, copyright © Augsburg Fortress.

Thanks be to you, O God, for Jesus Christ, who by the cross showed your great love for us in that he died for unbelievers.

Thanks be to you, O God, who in Jesus Christ calls us to take up the cross and follow him. Grant that we may joyfully answer the call and in truth become his disciples; in his name we pray. Amen.

God be in our minds, and in our understanding;
God be in our eyes, and in our seeing;
God be in our mouths, and in our speaking;
God be in our hearts, and in our thinking;
God be at our end, and at our departing. Amen.

Old Sarum Primer, adapted

The Service of Tenebrae

The term *tenebrae* comes from the practice of gradually extinguishing candles in the course of the service until all is in darkness. The worshipers then usually depart in silence. Choices from this order of Scripture readings may be used to frame a Maundy Thursday, Good Friday, or Easter Vigil service. Appropriate hymns or other music may be interspersed among the readings.

The Shadow of Betrayal	Matthew 26:20-25
The Shadow of Desertion	Matthew 26:31-35
The Agony of the Soul	Luke 22:39-44
The Unshared Vigil	Mark 14:32-41
"God, the hour is come"	John 17:1-6
"That they may all be one"	John 17:15-22
The Arrest at the Garden	John 18:1-5
The Shadow of the Cross	Mark 15:16-20
The Way of the Cross	Mark 15:21-32
"Truly, this was the Son of God!"	Mark 15:33-39

Easter

The great festival of Easter and the season that follows celebrates
Christ as the Savior of humanity and the Lord of all. It is a time
of joyful celebration and focuses on our continuing life of union
with Christ.

Sentences

The stone that the builders rejected has become the cornerstone; this was God's doing, and it is amazing in our eyes.
Matthew 21:42

Jesus came and stood among them and said to them,
"Peace be with you." After he said this, he showed them
his hands and his side. Then the disciples rejoiced when
they saw the Lord.
John 20:19-20

Christ, our paschal lamb, has been sacrificed. Therefore,
let us celebrate the festival, not with the old yeast, the
yeast of malice and evil, but with the unleavened bread of
sincerity and truth.
1 Corinthians 5:7-8

If then you have been raised with Christ, seek the things
that are above, where Christ is, seated at the right hand of
God.
Colossians 3:1

Christ holds his priesthood permanently, because he continues forever. Consequently he is able for all time to save
those who approach God through him, since he always
lives to make intercession for them.
Hebrews 7:24-25

Let us run with perseverance the race that is set before us, looking to Jesus the pioneer and perfecter of our faith, who for the sake of the joy that was set before him endured the cross, disregarding its shame, and has taken his seat at the right hand of the throne of God. Hebrews 12:1-2

Blessed be the God and Father of our Lord Jesus Christ! By God's great mercy we have been given a new birth into a living hope through the resurrection of Jesus Christ from the dead. 1 Peter 1:3

"I am the first and the last," says the Lord. "I am the living one. I was dead, and see, I am alive forever and ever." Revelation 1:17-18

The Lord has risen!
The Lord has risen indeed: Hallelujah!
Jesus said: "I am the resurrection and the life. Those who believe in me, even though they die, will live,
And everyone who lives and believes in me will never die." John 11:25-26

Christ, being raised from the dead, will never die again;
Death no longer has dominion over him.
The death he died, he died to sin, once for all;
But the life he lives, he lives to God.
So you also must consider yourselves dead to sin,
For we are alive to God in Jesus Christ.
Romans 6:9-11

Christ has been raised from the dead, the first fruits of those who have died.
Thanks be to God, who gives us the victory through our Lord Jesus Christ. 1 Corinthians 15:20,57

Prayers

Praise be to you, our Creator, who brought forth your Son from the dead and has raised him to eternal glory. Praise be to you, O Jesus Christ, who is the resurrection and the life. Praise be to you, O Holy Spirit, who makes God alive in our hearts. All praise and thanksgiving be to you, O most blessed Trinity, now and forever, world without end. **Amen.**

Our God, as we stand before the empty tomb, like Mary and the disciples we find it hard to believe that Christ rose from the dead. Forgive our unbelief. Take from our minds the shadows of doubt and help us to find in the midst of this world the Spirit of the living Christ. **Amen.**

We give thanks to you, O God, who has brought from the dead our Savior, Jesus Christ. Give us grace to believe in his victory and faith to make it our own. Help us every day to be more ready to minister than to be ministered to. Make us brave to fight for justice and to stand firm against those who would oppress others. In all our ways may we say with Christ, ''Not my will, but God's be done.'' Give us grace to know him as our living Lord and strength to follow in his footsteps; in his name we pray. **Amen.**

Almighty God, who by the death of your Son has destroyed sin and death, and by his resurrection has restored innocence and everlasting life in order that, delivered from the power of sin, we may live in your kingdom: grant that we may believe this with our whole heart, and, steadfast in this faith, may praise and thank you evermore; through Jesus Christ, our Savior. **Amen.**

Martin Luther, 1483–1546; adapted

Christ is risen:

The spirits of evil have fallen.

Christ is risen:

The angels of God are rejoicing.

Christ is risen:

The tomb is empty and still.

Christ has indeed arisen from the dead.

Glory and power are Christ's for ever and ever. Amen.

From an Easter hymn attributed to Hippolytus, adapted

The Lord has risen indeed:

Hallelujah!

Christ has been raised from the dead, the first fruits of those who have died.

Thanks be to God, who gives us the victory through our Lord Jesus Christ. Amen.

Rejoice, heavenly choirs of angels.

Rejoice, all creation around God's throne.

Jesus Christ, our King, is risen!

Sound the trumpet of salvation.

Rejoice, O earth, in shining splendor,

Radiant in the brightness of your King.

Christ has conquered! Glory fills you!

Darkness vanishes forever. Amen.

Our God, through the mighty resurrection of your son Jesus Christ you have liberated us from the power of darkness and brought us into the kingdom of your love; grant that as Christ was raised from the dead by your glory, so we may walk in newness of life and look for those things that are in heaven. In the name of Christ who is alive and reigns forever. **Amen.**   Gelasian Sacramentary, adapted

A hymn of glory let us sing;
New songs throughout the world shall ring:
   Alleluia! Alleluia!
Christ, by a road before untrod,
Ascended to the throne of God.
   Alleluia! Alleluia! Amen! The Venerable Bede, 673–735

Ascension

This day, the fortieth day after Easter, marks the exaltation of Christ as he takes his place at the right hand of God. Christ's ascension gives to us a share of his divinity and the promise of his continuing presence in our lives.

Sentences

God has gone up with a shout, the Lord with the sound of a trumpet. Sing praises to God, sing praises! Sing praises to our King, sing praises! God is the king of all the earth; sing praises with a psalm. God is king over the nations; God sits on a holy throne.   Psalm 47:5-8

Remember, I am with you always, to the end of the age.
                Matthew 28:20

So then the Lord Jesus, after he had spoken to them, was taken up into heaven and sat down at the right hand of God. And they went out and proclaimed the good news everywhere, while the Lord worked with them and confirmed the message by the signs that accompanied it.
                Mark 16:19-20

While Jesus was blessing them, he withdrew from them and was carried up into heaven. And they worshiped him, and returned to Jerusalem with great joy; and they were continually in the temple blessing God.   Luke 24:51-53

Jesus said, "And I, when I am lifted up from the earth, will draw all people to myself."   John 12:32

Thus it is written that the Messiah is to suffer and to rise from the dead on the third day,

That repentance and forgiveness of sins is to be proclaimed in his name to all nations.

You are witnesses of these things you have in Christ Jesus, who, though he was in the form of God, did not regard equality with God as something to be exploited,

But emptied himself, taking the form of a servant, being born in human likeness.

And being found in human form, he humbled himself and became obedient to the point of death—even death on a cross. Therefore God also highly exalted him and gave him the name that is above every name,

That at the name of Jesus every knee should bend and every tongue should confess that Jesus Christ is Lord.   Luke 24:46-48; Philippians 2:5-11

Prayers

Eternal God, with thanksgiving we come to Christ, that living stone rejected by the world but in your eyes chosen and precious, to offer our prayers and petitions. Grant that through him our unworthiness may find worth in your sight. May you who have called us also restore, establish, and strengthen us. To you be honor and glory forever and ever. **Amen.**

Since in Jesus Christ we have a great high priest who has ascended to the heavens, we confidently draw near to your throne of grace, our God. Grant us mercy and help us to find grace in time of need. May we come to know the presence of him who said: "Lo, I am with you always, even to the close of the age." **Amen.**

He who descended is also ascended far above the heavens, that he might fill all things.
> **When Christ, our Life, appears, we shall appear with him in glory. Alleluia! Amen!**

Pentecost

The day of Pentecost is witness and celebration to the pouring out of God's Spirit upon those who believe in Christ, and is observed in many churches as the birthday of the church.

Sentences

In the last days I will pour out my spirit on all flesh; your sons and your daughters shall prophesy, your old men shall dream dreams, and your young men shall see visions.

Joel 2:28

Jesus said to them, "Peace be with you. As God has sent me, so I send you." When he had said this, he breathed on them and said to them, "Receive the Holy Spirit. If you forgive the sins of any, they are forgiven them; if you retain the sins of any, they are retained." John 20:21-23

God's love has been poured into our hearts through the Holy Spirit that has been given to us. Romans 5:5

Do you not know that you are God's temple and that God's Spirit dwells in you?　　　　　　　　　　　　1 Corinthians 3:16

The fruit of the Spirit is love, joy, peace, patience, kindness, generosity, faithfulness, gentleness, and self-control. There is no law against such things. If we live by the Spirit, let us also be guided by the Spirit.　　　Galatians 5:22-23,25

The Spirit and the bride say, "Come." Let everyone who hears say, "Come." Let everyone who is thirsty come. Let anyone who wishes take the water of life as a gift.

Revelation 22:17

This is the day that God has made.
Let us rejoice and be glad in it.
This is the day of which Jesus declared: "You will receive power when the Holy Spirit has come upon you.

And you will be my witnesses in Jerusalem, in all Judea and Samaria, and to the ends of the earth."

Psalm 118:24; Acts 1:8

The hour is coming, and is now here, when the true worshipers will worship the Creator in spirit and truth, for the Creator seeks such as these.

God is spirit, and those who worship must worship in spirit and truth.　　　　　　　　　　　　John 4:23-24

Where the Spirit of the Lord is, there is freedom.
There are varieties of gifts, but the same Spirit.
For all who are led by the Spirit of God are children of God.

It is that very Spirit bearing witness with our spirit that we are the children of God.　　　　Romans 8:14,16

1 Corinthians 12:4

Prayers

Spirit of truth, Spirit of love, Spirit of Christ, Spirit of God, the Holy Spirit, we honor you for your many gifts to us. Fire our hearts and touch our lips, that we may sing forth praise worthy of your great power. **Amen.**

God, we offer to you praise for the gift of your Spirit. When we are lonely the Spirit comes to be our friend. When we are filled with doubt and lack faith the Spirit speaks the Word of truth. When we are filled with hatred the Spirit brings to us the gift of love. For your Spirit we praise you, O God our Redeemer. **Amen.**

Pour forth your Spirit, O God, on all the earth, that conflict and strife may be brought to an end. Deliver people everywhere from contempt for those who are of a different race, color, or creed. Hasten true fellowship among all peoples through your gospel, and bring them to true unity in your Spirit; through Jesus Christ our Lord. **Amen.**

Fire of the Spirit, life of the lives of creatures,
spiral of sanctity, bond of all natures,
glow of charity, lights of clarity, taste
of sweetness to sinners, be with us and hear us. . . .
Composer of all things, light of all the risen,
key of salvation, release from the dark prison,
hope of all unions, scope of chastities, joy
in the glory, strong honor, be with us and hear us. **Amen.**
      Hildegarde, twelfth century (trans. Charles Williams)

O heavenly Creator, we pray for your holy church universal. Send down upon its ministers and people your Holy

Spirit; give to them wisdom and grace; enlighten them with the knowledge of your Word; inflame them with a pure zeal for your glory. Grant that by their faithful witness and work your church may be strengthened and your kingdom made known in the world.

Hear our prayer, O God.

Grant your blessing to all those who translate, print, and circulate the Holy Scriptures; may your Spirit inspire them with true knowledge and skill, with patience and love.

Hear our prayer, O God.

Strengthen with your Spirit all our brothers and sisters, your servants in mission. Make them strong in your truth and love, help them to set forth Christ as the means to salvation.

Hear our prayer, O God. Amen.

Glory to you, O God, glory to you!
Heavenly Ruler, Comforter, Spirit of truth,
   Come and dwell within us.
You who are everywhere and who fills all things,
Treasury of all good and giver of life,
   Come, Holy Spirit, and dwell among us.
Cleanse us from all sin
And through your goodness, redeem our souls.
   Come, Holy Spirit, and dwell among us. Amen.

Orthodox prayer, adapted

Spirit divine, attend our prayers,
And make this house your home;
Descend with all your gracious powers;
O come, great Spirit, come!
   Come as the dove and spread your wings,
   The wings of peaceful love;

And let the church on earth become
Blest as the church above. Amen.

Andrew Reed, 1787–1862; adapted

Trinity/Kingdomtide

Green, the liturgical color of this long season, symbolizes that the season of the Sundays following Pentecost is a time for spiritual growth and study in the congregation. The emphasis is on Jesus' teachings about the kingdom of God, as well as themes of social justice and the mission of the church.

Sentences

Yours, O Lord, are the greatness, the power, the glory, the victory, and the majesty; for all that is in the heavens and on the earth is yours; yours is the kingdom, O God, and you are exalted as head above all.   1 Chronicles 29:11

Holy, holy, holy is the Lord of hosts; the whole earth is full of God's glory.   Isaiah 6:3

Strive first for the kingdom of God and God's righteousness, and all things will be given to you as well.

Matthew 6:33

The time is fulfilled, and the kingdom of God has come near; repent, and believe in the good news.   Mark 1:15

The grace of Jesus Christ, the love of God and the communion of the Holy Spirit be with all of you.

2 Corinthians 13:13

Through Christ we have access in one Spirit to God.

Ephesians 2:18

God has rescued us from the power of darkness and transferred us into the kingdom of God's beloved Son, in whom we have redemption, the forgiveness of sins.

Colossians 1:13-14

Let the word of Christ dwell in you richly; teach and admonish one another in all wisdom; and with gratitude in your hearts sing psalms, hymns, and spiritual songs to God.

Colossians 3:16

Therefore, brothers and sisters, be all the more eager to confirm your call as chosen ones, for if you do this, you will never stumble. For in this way, entry into the eternal kingdom of our Savior Jesus Christ will be richly provided for you.

2 Peter 1:10-11

But you, beloved, build yourselves up on your most holy faith; pray in the Holy Spirit; keep yourselves in the love of God; look forward to the mercy of our Lord Jesus Christ that leads to eternal life.

Jude 20-21

"I am the Alpha and the Omega," says God, who is and who was and who is to come, the Almighty.   Revelation 1:8

Rejoice in God, O you righteous. Praise befits the upright.
For the word of God is upright, and God's work is done in faithfulness.
God loves righteousness and justice; the earth is full of the steadfast love of God.
By the word of God the heavens were made, and all their host by the breath of God's mouth.

Our soul waits for God, who is our help and shield.

Let your steadfast love, O God, be upon us, even as we hope in you.   Psalm 33:1,4-6,20,22

God is our refuge and strength, a very present help in trouble.

Therefore we will not fear, though the earth should change, though the mountains tremble with its tumult.

There is a river whose streams make glad the city of God, the holy habitation of the Most High.

God is in the midst of the city; it shall not be moved. God will help it when the morning dawns.

The nations are in an uproar, the kingdoms totter; God utters a word, the earth melts.

The Lord of hosts is with us; the God of Jacob is our refuge.   Psalm 46:1-7

How lovely is your dwelling place, O God of hosts!

My soul longs, indeed it faints for the courts of God.

I would rather be a doorkeeper in the house of my God than live in tents of wickedness.

For God is a sun and shield; God bestows favor and honor.

No good thing does God withhold from those who walk uprightly.

Happy is everyone who trusts in you, O God.

          Psalm 84:1-2,10-12

Put away falsehood, then, and let all of us speak the truth to our neighbors, for we are members of one another.

We may be angry but we must not sin, nor let the sun go down on our anger.

Let no evil talk come out of our mouths, but only what is useful for building up, as there is need, so that our words may give grace to those who hear.

Let us put away all bitterness, wrath, anger, and slander, and be kind to one another, forgiving one another, as God in Christ has forgiven us.

Therefore may we be imitators of God, as beloved children,

And live in love, as Christ loved us and gave himself up for us. Ephesians 4:25-26,29,31-32;5:1-2

The saying is sure: if we have died with him, we will also live with him;

If we endure, we will also reign with him;

If we deny him, he will also deny us;

If we are faithless, he remains faithful.

2 Timothy 2:11-13

Prayers

Creator, Christ, and Holy Spirit, one God, we adore you for the many ways in which you have made yourself known to humanity. Heighten our thanksgiving, that it may be worthy of your greatness, and help us to sing your praises, that all the world may truly know how great you are. **Amen.**

Almighty and everlasting God, by whose Spirit the whole body of Christ is administered and blessed, receive our supplications and prayers which we offer before you for all ministers of your church, that every member of that vocation may serve you in truth and godliness; through our Savior, Jesus Christ. **Amen.**

We rejoice, O God, in your marvelous works, the works of your hand. To you it is most fitting to offer our thanks and declare your steadfast love in the morning and your faithfulness by night. We give to you the praise, O God; for you shall all our earthly work be performed. **Amen.**

Our God, we your servants gather in your presence to be strengthened and healed, inspired and empowered so that our work may make your compassion known. Speak to us, so that we may be a community that celebrates and proclaims your redemptive work. May we be ever faithful to our call, always acting with conviction. We ask this in the name of Jesus Christ, our Redeemer. **Amen.**

O God, by the gift of your Spirit establish and ground us in your truth. Reveal to us what we do not know; make perfect in us what is lacking; strengthen us in what we do know; and keep us ever in your service, through Jesus Christ. **Amen.**   Clement of Rome, adapted

Lord, heavenly Creator, in whom is the fullness of light and wisdom, enlighten our minds by your Holy Spirit, and give us grace to receive your Word with reverence and humility, without which no one can understand your truth. For Christ's sake, we pray. **Amen.**

John Calvin, 1509–1564; adapted

Why are we gathered at this place at this hour?
We are gathered as the people of God, to come to know and serve and praise God as seen in Jesus Christ and made known by the Holy Spirit.
Then let us acknowledge the God before whom we stand.
In the name of the Creator and of the Christ and of the Holy Spirit. Amen.

Blessed be you, O eternal God:

In whom the heavens rejoice and the earth is glad, for you will judge the world in righteousness.

Blessed be you, O Christ our Savior:

Who will come in power and great glory to perfect God's kingdom, and bring home the ransomed with songs of everlasting joy.

Blessed be you, O holy and gracious Spirit:

Who quickens our hearts and fill our mouths with praise.

Glory be to you, O God, who is one yet three, forever and ever. **Amen.**

Let us give glory to God.

Glory be to the Creator, and to the Son, and to the Holy Spirit.

As it was in the beginning, is now and ever shall be,

World without end. Amen.

The Lord be with you.

And with your spirit.

Beloved in Christ, in communion with the saints of all ages let us boldly offer our prayers of intercession to almighty God: Creator, Christ, and Holy Spirit.

O God, we pray for the church, which is set amid the confusion of contemporary life and is face-to-face with a great new task.

Be with your church, O God.

Grant the church a new birth through the labor of repentance. Put upon its lips the ancient gospel of God.

Be with your church, O God.

Help it to boldly proclaim the coming of the kingdom of God.

Be with your church, O God.

Fill it with the prophet's scorn of tyranny, and with a Christlike tenderness for the burdened and the oppressed. Give it faith to defend the cause of the people.

Be with your church, O God.

Let it cease from seeking its own life, lest that life be lost. Make it courageous to give up its life to humanity, as did the crucified Christ, in whose name we pray.

Be with your church, O God. Amen.

God of the outcast and the oppressed, we entrust to you all who are sick, in danger, in sorrow; all little children; all the elderly.

By your Spirit hear our prayers, O merciful and gracious God, for the love of your Son, our Savior Jesus Christ.

Let the sorrowful sighing of the prisoners come before you, and according to the greatness of your power comfort those who are preparing to die.

By your Spirit hear our prayers, O merciful and gracious God, for the love of your Son, our Savior Jesus Christ. Amen.

Almighty and gracious God, we pray that you would sow the seed of your Word in our hearts,

Send down upon us your heavenly grace;

That we may bring forth the fruits of the Spirit,

And on the great day of harvest be gathered with your saints; through Jesus Christ we pray. Amen.

Canterbury Convocation of 1862, adapted

We thank you, our God, for the life and knowledge that you have made known to us through Jesus Christ, your servant.

To God be glory forever!

As the broken bread, once scattered upon the mountains, has been gathered together and made one, so may your church be gathered together from the ends of the earth into one kingdom;

To God be the glory and the power through Jesus Christ forever! Amen.

The Didache, second century, adapted

All the way our Savior leads us
Cheers each winding path we tread,
Gives us grace for every trial,
Feeds us with the living bread.
Though our weary steps may falter
And our souls may thirsty be,
Gushing from the Rock before us,
Lo! a spring of joy we see.

Fanny Crosby, 1820–1915; adapted

Part 4

Sentences, Scriptures, and Prayers for Special Days and Occasions

While these days and occasions do not belong to the Christian liturgical year, they have become a part of the recurring cycle of the church's worship. They provide occasions wherein the church reminds itself of God's special mercies, as well as of its own involvement in human society.

New Year

Sentences

The eyes of the Lord your God are always upon you, from the beginning of the year to the end of the year.

Deuteronomy 11:12

God, you have been our dwelling place in all generations. Before the mountains were brought forth, or ever you had formed the earth and the world, from everlasting to everlasting you are God. Psalm 90:1-2

Teach us to count our days that we may gain a wise heart. Satisfy us in the morning with your steadfast love, so that we may rejoice and be glad all our days. Let the favor of God be upon us, and prosper for us the work of our hands—O prosper the work of our hands!

Psalm 90:12,14,17

For a thousand years in your sight are like yesterday when it is past, or like a watch in the night. You sweep them away; they are like a dream, like grass that is renewed in the morning; in the morning it flourishes and is renewed; in the evening it fades and withers.   Psalm 90:4-6

Those who wait for God shall renew their strength, they shall mount up with wings like eagles, they shall run and not be weary, they shall walk and not faint.   Isaiah 40:31

Thus says our God: ''I am about to do a new thing; now it springs forth, do you not perceive it? I will make a way in the wilderness and rivers in the desert.''   Isaiah 43:19

Jesus said: ''Therefore I tell you, do not worry about your life, what you will eat, or about your body, what you will wear. For life is more than food and the body more than clothing. Can any of you by worrying add a single hour to your span of life? For it is the nations of the world that strive after all these things, and God knows that you need them. Instead, strive for God's kingdom, and these things will be given to you as well.''   Luke 12:22-23,25,30-31

We do not lose heart. Though our outer nature is wasting away, our inner nature is being renewed day by day. We look not at what can be seen; for what can be seen is temporary, but what cannot be seen is eternal.

2 Corinthians 4:16,18

If anyone is in Christ, there is a new creation: everything old has passed away; see, everything has become new! All this is from God, who reconciled us to himself through Christ, and has given us the ministry of reconciliation.

2 Corinthians 5:17-18

The one who was seated on the throne said, "See, I am making all things new. I am the Alpha and the Omega, the beginning and the end. To the thirsty I will give water as a gift from the spring of the water of life. Those who conquer will inherit these things, and I will be their God and they will be my children."　　　　Revelation 21:5-7

O God, our God, how majestic is your name in all the earth!

When we look at your heavens, the work of your fingers, the moon and the stars you have established, what are human beings that you are mindful of them?

Yet you have made us a little lower than the divine beings, and crowned us with glory and honor.

You have given us dominion over the works of your hands; you have put all things under our feet,

All sheep and oxen, and also the beasts of the field, the birds of the air, and the fish of the sea.

O God, our God, how majestic is your name in all the earth!　　　　Psalm 8

I lift my eyes to the hills—from where will my help come?

Our help comes from God, who made heaven and earth.

God will not let your foot be moved; the one who keeps you will not slumber.

The one who keeps Israel will neither slumber nor sleep.

God is your keeper, God is your shade at your right hand.

The sun shall not strike us by day, nor the moon by night.

God will keep you from all evil; God will keep your life.

God will keep our going out and our coming in from this time on and forevermore.   Psalm 121

See, now is the acceptable time; see, now is the day of salvation!

For we are the temple of the living God;

As God said,

"I will live in them and walk among them,
and I will be their God,
and they shall be my people.

Since we have these promises, let us cleanse ourselves from every defilement of body and spirit, making holiness perfect in the fear of God.

2 Corinthians 6:2,16;7:1

Scripture Selections

Genesis 1:1–2:3. Deuteronomy 8. Job 36; 37; 38. Psalm 1; 8; 19; 25; 27; 29; 34; 39; 46; 57:7-11; 62; 90; 91; 102:25-28; 103; 121; 130; 139; 146. Proverbs 3:1-18. Isaiah 40:21-31. Matthew 6:25-34; 25:14-30; 25:31-46. Luke 12:22-48. 2 Corinthians 5:1-10. Ephesians 6:10-20. Hebrews 11; 12:18-29. 1 Peter 1:1-25. 2 Peter 3:8-18.

Prayers

As this old year passes, O God, we acknowledge your presence as ruler not only of the past but also of the present and future; we acknowledge that you make all things new.

We ask you to use us as your instruments in your work in the world. Empower us through your grace, that through knowledge we may in the present search out your ways for the future. Make us strong witnesses to our faith. Use us, that others in despair may perceive hope in you. As we have received your love, may we in turn fulfill loving relationships with you, with our sisters and brothers, and with ourselves. May your kingdom come and your will be done; through Jesus Christ. **Amen.**

O God of holy love, we acknowledge that at the beginning of this year our lives do not stand before you as a book unwritten. Much that we will do has already been spelled out before the year has begun. Inscribed deep within are old habits and familiar behavior patterns. We know that these in large part will write for us the story of this coming year. As we live, make us aware of your forgiving grace, that we may write new life-pages and avoid the errors of the past. We ask this in the name of Jesus Christ. **Amen.**

O Christ, who is both Alpha and Omega, the beginning and the end, and whose years will not fail: grant us so to pass through the coming year with faithful hearts that in all things we may please you and glorify your name; who lives and reigns with the Creator and the Holy Spirit, ever one God, world without end. **Amen.**

Mozarabic Sacramentary, adapted

Eternal God, as another year draws to its close we give you thanks for all the ways by which you have led us. For your goodness that has created us, for your bounty that has sustained us, for your wise discipline that has corrected us, and for your patience that has supported us:
We thank you, O God.

For the worship and uplifting fellowship of your church, for the light and inspiration of your Word, and for the comfort and guidance of your Holy Spirit:

We thank you, O God.

For all the truth we have learned, for all the good you have enabled us to do, for all victories won and for all blessings of life:

We thank you, O God.

For Jesus Christ, who has called us into his way, his truth, and his life, and has shown us your holy love:

We thank you, O God, to whom be all praise and thanksgiving, now and forevermore. Amen.

Ageless God, who laid the foundations of the earth, and whose mercy is from everlasting to everlasting, in this beginning of the new year we raise our voices in thanksgiving to you. For the old, which we cherish and hold dear:

We praise your name; we give you thanks.

For the new, with its untold promise and its possibilities:

We praise your name; we give you thanks.

For your strength that sustains us when we are weak, for your patience that bears with when we sin, for your guidance that leads us when we are confused, and for your comfort that helps us when we are in distress:

We praise your name; we give you thanks.

Most of all, for your forgiveness and grace in Jesus Christ, for the abiding presence of your Holy Spirit, for our fellowship with you and with one another, and for our assurance of eternal life in your heavenly kingdom:

We praise your name; we give you thanks.

Therefore we worship and adore you, O Lord our God.

To God be glory forever and ever. Amen.

Great God, we sing that mighty hand
By which supported still we stand;
The opening year your mercy shows;
May mercy crown it till it close.
With grateful hearts the past we own;
The future, all to us unknown,
We to your guardian care commit,
And peaceful leave before your feet. Amen.

Philip Doddridge, 1702–1751

Missions: Home and Abroad

Sentences

The people who walked in darkness have seen a great light;
those who lived in a land of deep darkness—on them light
has shined. Isaiah 9:2

Thus says God, "I am your God, I have called you in
righteousness, I have taken you by the hand and kept you;
I have given you as a covenant to the people, a light to the
nations, to open the eyes that are blind, to bring out the
prisoners from the dungeon, from the prison those who sit
in darkness." Isaiah 42:6-7

How beautiful upon the mountains are the feet of the messenger who announces peace, who brings good news, who
announces salvation, who says to Zion, "Your God
reigns." Isaiah 52:7

Jesus said: "The harvest is plentiful, but the laborers are
few; therefore ask the Creator of the harvest to send out
laborers into this harvest." Matthew 9:37

Jesus said: "All authority in heaven and on earth has been given to me. Go therefore and make disciples of all nations, baptizing them in the name of the Creator and of the Son and of the Holy Spirit, and teaching them to obey everything that I have commanded you. And remember, I am with you always, to the end of the age."

Matthew 28:18-20

Jesus said: "Go into all the world and proclaim the good news to the whole creation. The one who believes and is baptized will be saved." Mark 16:15-16

Jesus said: "I am the light of the world. Whoever follows me will never walk in darkness but will have the light of life." John 8:12

Jesus said: "I have other sheep that do not belong to this fold. I must bring them also, and they will listen to my voice. So there will be one flock, one shepherd."

John 10:16

From one ancestor God made all nations to inhabit the whole earth, and he allotted the times of their existence and the boundaries of the places where they would live, so that they would search for God and perhaps grope for him and find him—though indeed he is not far from each one of us. For "In God we live and move and have our being." Acts 17:26-28

Bear one another's burdens, and in this way you will fulfill the law of Christ. So then, whenever we have an opportunity, let us work for the good of all, and especially for those of the family of faith. Galatians 6:2,10

God looks down from heaven, seeing all humankind. God watches all the inhabitants of the earth, fashions their hearts, and observes their deeds.

Truly the eye of God is on those who fear God, on those who hope in God's steadfast love.

Our soul waits for God, who is our help and shield. We have a glad heart because we trust in God's holy name.

Let your steadfast love, O God, be upon us, even as we hope in you. Psalm 33:13-15,18-22

O God, you are enthroned forever; your name endures to all generations. You will rise up and have compassion on Zion, for it is time to favor it. For your servants hold its stones dear, and have pity on its dust.

O God, you are enthroned forever; your name endures to all generations.

The nations will fear the name of God, and all the rulers of earth your glory. For God will build up Zion. God will regard the prayer of the destitute, and will not despise their prayer.

O God, you are enthroned forever; your name endures to all generations.

Let this be recorded for a generation to come, so that a people yet unborn may praise God: that God looked down at the earth from the holy height, to hear the groans of the prisoners, to set free those who were doomed to die.

O God, you are enthroned forever; your name endures to all generations.

The name of God will be declared in Zion, and God's praise in Jerusalem, when peoples gather together to worship.

O God, you are enthroned forever; your name endures to all generations. Psalm 102:12-22

O give thanks to God, for God is good;

God's steadfast love endures forever.

Let the redeemed of God say so, those redeemed from trouble.

God's steadfast love endures forever.

Let the redeemed be gathered in from the lands, from the east and from the west, from the north and from the south.

God's steadfast love endures forever.

For God satisfies the thirsty, and the hungry are filled with good things.

God's steadfast love endures forever.

Some sat in darkness and in gloom; they cried to God in their trouble, and God brought them out and broke their bonds asunder.

God's steadfast love endures forever.

Let those who are wise give heed to these things, and consider the unfailing love of God.

God's steadfast love endures forever.

Psalm 107:1-3,9-14,43

Scripture Selections

Genesis 12:1-9. Psalm 46; 67; 107; 126. Isaiah 6; 42:1-13; 49:1-13; 55; 60:1-7. Jeremiah 1:1-10. Ezekiel 37:1-14. Jonah 1; 3. Malachi 3. Matthew 9:35–10:16; 28:16-20. Luke 10:1-22. John 1:35-51; 17:2-26; 20:19-23. Acts 1:1-19; 8; 16:9-15; 17:22-34. Romans 10:1-17; 12; 15:14-33. 1 Corinthians 9; 12. 2 Corinthians 5:11-21; 8; 9. Galatians 6. 1 John 4:7-21.

Prayers

Too often, God, we have tried to be Christian with our words alone and have forgotten that the disciples of Jesus Christ are known also by their fruits. We have praised you within the sanctuary while on the streets we have walked past human need. We have spoken of mission but forgotten that Christ went into all the cities, villages, and towns of his home country to preach the gospel, heal the sick, and comfort the sorrowing. Forgive us, God, that we have neglected so great a task; and grant that through Jesus Christ we may become disciples in deed as well as word. **Amen.**

We thank you, God, for Jesus Christ, who in the days of his earthly ministry saw fit to walk the crowded streets of the city and the narrow paths of the countryside, and there to minister to human need. We thank you that he called his disciples into that same ministry and that even now men and women are serving in his name amidst the poverty and despair of the cities, as well as in other places where human need is overwhelming. We thank you that even though we cannot stand beside these missionaries we can have a part in their ministry through our prayers and by sharing with them of our substance. We thank you for those in our land whose vision and work has brought the light of the gospel to all conditions of humanity. Accept our thanksgivings in Christ's name. **Amen.**

We ask, O God, your blessing upon all those who have dedicated their lives to Christ's mission in our land. As they work in cities, on reservations, in local churches, in schools and colleges, and in whatever places you have called them, we pray that their insight and strength may continue to deepen and their dedication and labor may continue to bring the Word of peace to those with whom they minister. We ask in the name of the one who called all people to be his witnesses, in Jerusalem and Judea and to the uttermost parts of the earth. **Amen.**

Eternal God, you made the world and everything in it. You gave to all humankind life and breath and made from one woman and one man every nation on earth. We praise you and thank you for the calling you give to those who are special witnesses to the marvels of your grace. We thank you for prophets and apostles who have in times past spoken your truth, and for the ambassadors of Christ in every age who have gone forth into distant lands to bring light and healing to those who dwell in darkness and in the shadow of death. Above all, we thank you for Jesus Christ, whom you sent as your witness in the world and who has given us the hope that the kingdoms of this world will become your kingdom, with all sharing in peace and love. **Amen.**

Remember in your mercy, God, all who are your children. Let the whole earth be filled with your praise and made glad by the knowledge of your name.

> **May they proclaim the good news and be a light to the nations.**

Be with all missionaries who this day are working in distant lands. Help them to come to know the ways and words of the people with whom they serve. Keep them ever open to the people around them.

> **May they proclaim the good news and be a light to the nations.**

Help them to know when they should speak and when they should remain silent. Grant them the grace and humility to learn from those whom they are teaching.

> **May they proclaim the good news and be a light to the nations.**

Let them be ready and willing to commit into the hands of those with whom they labor the care and leadership of your church, the church of Jesus Christ.

May they proclaim the good news and be a light to the nations. Amen.

Hark! the voice of Jesus crying,
"Who will go and work today?
Fields are white and harvests waiting,
Who will bear the sheaves away?"
Loud and long the Master calls us,
Rich reward he offers free;
Who will answer, gladly saying,
"Here am I, send me, send me"? Amen.

Daniel March, 1816–1909

Christian Education and Youth

Sentences

Happy are those whose delight is in the law of God; on God's law they meditate day and night. They are like trees planted by streams of water, which yield their fruit in its season, and their leaves do not wither. In all that they do, they prosper.

Psalm 1:1-3

We bless God who gives us counsel; in the night also our hearts instruct us. We keep God always before us; because God is at our right hand, we shall not be moved. You show us the path of life. In your presence there is fullness of joy; in your right hand are pleasures forevermore.

Psalm 16:7-8,11

Who shall ascend the hill of God? And who shall stand in that holy place? Those who have clean hands and pure hearts, who do not lift up their souls to what is false, and do not swear deceitfully. They will receive blessing from God, and vindication from the God of their salvation.

Psalm 24:3-5

We are like green olive trees in the house of God. We trust in the steadfast love of God forever and ever. We will thank you forever for what you have done. In the presence of the faithful we will proclaim your name, for it is good.

Psalm 52:8-9

How can young people keep their way pure? By guarding it according to your word. With our whole hearts we seek you; do not let us stray from your commandments. We treasure your word in our hearts, so that we may not sin against you. Blessed are you, O God; teach us your statutes. With our lips we declare all the ordinances of your mouth. We delight in the way of your decrees as much as in all riches. We will meditate on your precepts, and fix our eyes on your ways. We will delight in your statutes; we will not forget your word.

Psalm 119:9-16

God gives wisdom and from God's mouth come knowledge and understanding; God stores up sound wisdom for the upright and is a shield to those who walk blamelessly, guarding the paths of justice and preserving the ways of the faithful.

Proverbs 2:6-8

Trust in God with all your heart, and do not rely on your own insight. In all your ways acknowledge God, and God will make straight your paths.

Proverbs 3:5-6

Keep hold of instruction, do not let go; guard her, for she is your life.

Proverbs 4:13

The child grew and became strong, filled with wisdom; and the favor of God was upon him. Luke 2:40

You then, my child, be strong in the grace that is in Christ Jesus; and what you have heard from me through many witnesses entrust to faithful people who will be able to teach others as well. 2 Timothy 2:1-2

Do your best to present yourself to God as one approved by God, a worker who has no need to be ashamed, rightly explaining the word of truth. 2 Timothy 2:15

Teach what is consistent with sound doctrine. Show yourself in all respects a model of good works, and in your teaching show integrity, gravity, and sound speech.

Titus 2:1,7-8

Make us to know your ways, O God; teach us your paths.
Lead us in your truth, God, and teach us.
For you are the God of our salvation; for you we wait all day long.
Lead us in your truth, God, and teach us.
Be mindful of your mercy, O God, and of your steadfast love, for they have been from of old.
Lead us in your truth, God, and teach us.
Do not remember the sins of our youth or our transgressions; according to your steadfast love remember us, for your goodness' sake!
Lead us in your truth, God, and teach us. Psalm 25:4-7

For learning about wisdom and instruction, for understanding words of insight,
For gaining instruction in wise dealing, righteousness, justice, and equity;

To teach shrewdness to the innocent, knowledge and prudence to the young,

Let the wise also hear and gain in learning, and the discerning acquire skill,

Understanding proverbs and figures, the words of the wise and their riddles.

The fear of God is the beginning of knowledge.

Proverbs 1:2-7

Scripture Selections

Exodus 20:1-17. 1 Samuel 12:19-25. 1 Kings 3:5-9. Psalm 19; 26; 34. Proverbs 1:1-9. Jeremiah 31:31-37. Micah 6:6-8. Matthew 5:1-11; 6:5-14; 19:13-27. Luke 11:9-13. Philippians 2:1-11. 2 Timothy 2:1-15. Titus 2:1-8. Hebrews 2:1-4; 12. 1 Peter 1:3-9. 1 John 1:1-4; 3:1-3.

Prayers

In times past, O God, you taught through your holy prophets your will and your way. We praise you that your voice has not grown silent, but that you have given us teachers to open before us your truth and to lead us into right paths. Continue to lead us, we pray, through Christ. **Amen.**

God's Word is our great heritage
And shall be ours forever;
To spread its light from age to age
Shall be our chief endeavor.
Through life it guides our way;
In death it is our stay.
Lord, grant while time shall last

Your Church may hold it fast
Throughout all generations. **Amen.**

Nikolai Grundtvig, 1783–1872

Merciful and gracious God, hear the thanksgivings with which we come before you, in the name of Jesus Christ. For your providence that sustains and supports us; for your love that chastens and heals us:
  We thank you God, our Creator.
For minds that make us restless until we know the truth; for faith that promises triumph over doubt:
  We thank you God, our Creator.
For fleeting glimpses of reality, for visions we cannot describe, for depths we can but feel:
  We thank you God, our Creator.
For the labor of scholars that adds to our understanding; for the inspiration we receive from those of simple trust:
  We thank you God, our Creator.
For all who are faithful teachers of your truth; and especially those who have taught us to know and understand your way:
  We thank you God, our Creator.
For the writers and publishers of books and magazines which help those who teach and those who learn to come to a clearer understanding of your Word:
  We thank you God, our Creator.
For all these blessings which you have given, that we might use them wisely and well:
  We thank you God, our Creator. Amen.

Lord, speak to us, that we may speak
In living echoes of your tone;
As you have sought, so let us seek
Your straying children, lost and lone.

Oh, teach us, Lord, that we may teach
The precious truths which you impart;
And wing our words, that they may reach
The hidden depths of many a heart. Amen.

Frances Havergal, 1836–1879; adapted

Christian Home and Family Life

Sentences

Honor your father and your mother, so that your days may
be long in the land that your God is giving you.

Exodus 20:12

Hear, O Israel: The Lord is our God, the Lord alone. You
shall love God with all your heart, and with all your soul,
and with all your might. Keep these words that I am com-
manding you today in your heart. Recite them to your children and talk about them when you are at home and when
you are away, when you lie down and when you rise.

Deuteronomy 6:4-7

Now therefore revere God, and serve God in sincerity and
in faithfulness. Choose this day whom you will serve,
whether the gods your ancestors served or the gods of the
land in which you are living; but as for me and my household, we will serve God.   Joshua 24:14-15

Unless God builds the house, those who build it labor in
vain.   Psalm 127:1

We will tell of your name to our brothers and sisters; in the
midst of the congregation we will praise you: you who fear

God, praise God! All you offspring of Jacob, glorify God; stand in awe of God, all you offspring of Israel! Posterity will serve God; future generations will be told about God, and proclaim God's deliverance to a people yet unborn.

Psalm 22:22-23,30-31

O God, from our youth you have taught us, and we still proclaim your wondrous deeds. So even to old age and gray hairs, O God, do not forsake us, until we proclaim your might to all generations to come.   Psalm 71:17-18

Give ear, O my people, to my teaching; incline your ears to the words of my mouth. I will open my mouth in a parable; I will utter dark sayings from of old, things that we have heard and known, that our ancestors have told us. We will not hide them from their children; we will tell to the coming generation the glorious deeds of God and the wonders that God has done.   Psalm 78:1-4

We will sing of your steadfast love, O God, forever; with our mouths we will proclaim your faithfulness to all generations. We declare that your steadfast love is established forever; your faithfulness is as firm as the heavens. You said, ''I have made a covenant with my chosen one, I have sworn to my servant David: I will establish your descendants forever, and build your throne for all generations.''

Psalm 89:1-4

A wise child makes a glad father, but a foolish child is a mother's grief.   Proverbs 10:1

Jesus said, ''Let the little children come to me, and do not stop them; for it is to such as these that the kingdom of heaven belongs.''   Matthew 19:14

Love is patient; love is kind; love is not envious or boastful or arrogant or rude. It does not insist on its own way; it is not irritable or resentful; it does not rejoice in wrongdoing, but rejoices in truth. Love bears all things, believes all things, hopes all things, endures all things. Love never ends. 1 Corinthians 13:4-8

Praise God! Happy are those who fear God, who greatly delight in God's commandments.
> **Their descendants will be mighty in the land; the generation of the upright will be blessed.**

Wealth and riches are in their houses, and their righteousness endures forever.
> **They rise in the darkness as a light for the upright; they are gracious, merciful, and righteous.**

It is well with those who deal generously and lend, who conduct their affairs with justice.
> **The righteous will never be moved; they will be remembered forever.**

They have distributed freely, they have given to the poor;
> **Their righteousness endures forever.** Psalm 112:1-6,9

Happy is everyone who fears God, who walks in God's ways.
> **They shall eat the fruit of the labor of their hands; they shall be happy, and it shall go well with them.**

The parents will be like fruitful vines within their house; their children will be like olive shoots around their table.
> **Thus shall the ones be blessed who fear God.**

May they see the prosperity of Jerusalem all the days of their lives.
> **May they see their children's children. Peace be upon Israel!** Psalm 128

Scripture Selections

Genesis 2:18-24. Deuteronomy 6:1-9. Psalm 128; 145. Proverbs 31: 10-31. Mark 9:14-29. Luke 1:46-55; 2:41-52; 15:11-31. John 17. 1 Corinthians 13. Hebrews 11:1-3,8-12; 13:1-6. 1 Peter 3:8-12. 1 John 5:1-11.

Prayers

Gracious God, our Parent, we thank you that you chose the humble home of a village carpenter to cradle the infant Jesus, and that in this home he grew and became strong, filled with wisdom, and that your favor was upon him. Grant that the love seen so plentifully in Mary and the care and concern of Joseph for the child Jesus may be in us, and that our children may grow and become strong, filled with wisdom, and may be in your favor. **Amen.**

On this day, our God, as we offer thanks for your gracious gift of home and family, we would remember: those who live in broken homes; those who do not know the strong love of a father or the gentle concern of a mother; those whose homes are afflicted with poverty, or damaged by alcoholism or drugs; those whose homes have everything of this world's goods but lack all spirituality. We ask you, loving God, that all homes and families may be strengthened by your grace, your love, and your protection. This we ask through Jesus Christ. **Amen.**

Then here will I and mine today
A solemn covenant make and say:
Though all the world forsake God's Word,
I and my house will serve the Lord. **Amen.**
   Christoph von Pfiel (Catherine Winkworth, trans.), 1712–1784

God, behold our family here assembled.
We thank you for this place in which we dwell,
for the love that unites us, for the peace accorded to us this day,
for the hope with which we expect the morrow;
for the health, the work, the food, and the bright skies that make our lives delightful;
for our friends in all parts of the earth.
Give us courage and gaiety and the quiet mind.
Spare us to our friends, soften us to our enemies.
Bless us, if it may be, in all our innocent endeavors; if it may not, give us the strength to endure that which is to come:
that we may be brave in peril, constant in tribulation, temperate in wrath and in all changes of fortune,
and down to the gates of death,
loyal and loving to one another.
We beseech of you this help and mercy for Christ's sake. Amen.   Robert Louis Stevenson, 1850–1894

God, teach us to work with love, knowing that work is love made visible.
Teach us to weave the cloth with threads drawn from our heart, even as if you, our beloved, were to wear that cloth.
To build a house with affection, even as if you were to dwell in that house.
To sow seeds with tenderness and reap the harvest with joy, even as if you were to eat the fruit.
To charge all things we fashion with a breath of our own spirit,

And to know that all who have gone before us are standing about us and watching.

Kahlil Gibran, 1883–1931; adapted

Church Anniversary

Sentences

O God, we love the house in which you dwell, and the place where your glory abides. Our feet stand on level ground; in the great congregation we will bless the name of God.   Psalm 26:8,12

These things we remember as we pour out our souls: how we went with the throng, and led them in procession to the house of God, with glad shouts and songs of thanksgiving, a multitude keeping festival.   Psalm 42:4

We ponder your steadfast love, O God, in the midst of your temple. Your name, O God, like your praise, reaches to the ends of the earth. Walk around Zion, go all around it, count its towers, consider well its ramparts; go through its citadels, that you may tell the next generation that this is God, our God forever and ever.   Psalm 48:9-10,12-14

I was glad when they said to me, "Let us go to the house of God!   Psalm 122:1

Enlarge the sight of your tent, and let the curtains of your habitations be stretched out; do not hold back; lengthen your cords and strengthen your stakes. For you will spread out to the right and to the left, and your descendants will possess the nations. Isaiah 54:2-3

Jesus said: "Where two or three are gathered in my name, I am there among them." Matthew 18:20

They were all together in one place. And they devoted themselves to the apostles' teaching and fellowship, to the breaking of bread and the prayers. Acts 2:1,42

No one can lay any foundation other than the one that has been laid; that foundation is Jesus Christ. Do you not know that you are God's temple and that God's Spirit dwells in you? 1 Corinthians 3:11,16

I thank my God every time I remember you, constantly praying with joy in every one of my prayers for all of you, because of your sharing in the gospel from the first day until now. I am confident of this, that the one who began a good work among you will bring it to completion by the day of Jesus Christ. This is my prayer, that your love may overflow more and more with knowledge and full insight to help you to determine what is best, so that in the day of Christ you may be pure and blameless, having produced the harvest of righteousness that comes through Jesus Christ for the glory and praise of God.

Philippians 1:3-6,9-11

Come to Jesus Christ, a living stone, though rejected by mortals yet chosen and precious in God's sight, and like living stones, let yourselves be built into a spiritual house, to be a holy priesthood, to offer spiritual sacrifices acceptable to God through Jesus Christ. 1 Peter 2:4-5

O God, you are our God, we seek you. We have looked upon you in the sanctuary, beholding your power and glory.

Because your steadfast love is better than life, our lips will praise you.

We will bless you as long as we live; we will lift up our hands and call on your name.

Our souls are satisfied as with a rich feast, and our mouths praise you with joyful lips. Psalm 63:1-5

How lovely is your dwelling place, O God of hosts!

Our souls long, indeed they faint for the courts of God; our hearts and our flesh sing for joy to the living God.

Even the sparrow finds a home and the swallow a nest for herself, where she may lay her young at your altars, O Lord of hosts.

Happy are we who live in your house, ever singing your praise.

For a day in your courts is better than a thousand elsewhere. I would rather be a doorkeeper in the house of my God than live in the tents of wickedness.

For God is a sun and shield; no good thing does God withhold from those who walk uprightly.

Psalm 84:1-4,10-11

Scripture Selections

Psalm 84; 100; 111; 118:19-29; 122; 133; 147. Jeremiah 31:31-34. Matthew 7:24-27; 16:13-28. John 10:1-18; 15:1-17; 17. Acts 2. Romans 12. 1 Corinthians 12. Ephesians 2; 3; 4:1-16. Colossians 3:1-17. Hebrews 10:19-25; 11. 1 Peter 2:1-10.

Prayers

Almighty God, who set the one foundation of every church, renew our human temple, that it may, through us, continue to serve you. Be with us in our tasks of decision making and program planning, that we may reflect the light of your spirit. Have mercy on us, that we may go boldly into the world preaching and teaching your Word. Grant that as we come to this time of celebration we will not be so involved with ourselves; let us see you and know your will. This we ask in the name of Jesus Christ. **Amen.**

To you, O God, who has built your church upon the one sure foundation, Jesus Christ, we lift up our hearts this day in gratitude. We give thanks for this day and the meaning it has in our lives. We thank you for the Word preached in this church, and for the symbols of our membership in the body of Christ. We thank you for the good fellowship of your people; and for the eternal blessing of grace which you have given us through Jesus Christ. We thank you for this church building, this whole congregation, and each of its members and friends. We bless your holy name for those who have established this community and built this house of prayer. To you, O God, be praise and glory in the church throughout all ages; through Jesus Christ. **Amen.**

O God, make the door of this house wide enough to receive all who need human love and fellowship; narrow enough to shut out all envy, pride and strife.
For you, O God, are the foundation of our days.
Make its threshold smooth enough to be no stumbling-block to children, nor to straying feet, but rugged and strong enough to turn back the tempter's power.
For you, O God, are the foundation of our days.

God, make the door of this house the gateway to your eternal kingdom.

For you, O God, are the foundation of our days.
Amen.   On St. Stephen's Walbrook, London; adapted

We are a house of living stones,
Built for God's own habitation;
  Filling our hearts, these humble thrones,
  Granting us life and salvation.
Through all the passing years, O God,
Grant that when church bells are ringing,
  Many may come to hear the Word
  Where God this promise is bringing. Amen.
                    Nikolai Grundtvig, 1783–1872; adapted

World-Wide Communion and Christian Unity

Sentences

Sing to God a new song; sing to God, all the earth. Sing and bless God's name; tell of salvation from day to day. Declare the glory of God among the nations and the marvelous works of God among all the peoples. Psalm 96:1-3

How very good and pleasant it is when kindred live together in unity.   Psalm 133:1

Jesus said, "I ask not only on behalf of these, but also on behalf of those who will believe in me through their word, that they may all be one. As you, God, are in me and I am in you, may they also be in us, so that the world may believe that you have sent me."   John 17:20-21

Day by day, as they spent much time together in the temple, they broke bread at home and ate their food with glad and generous hearts, praising God and having the goodwill of all the people.   Acts 2:46-47

Lead a life worthy of the calling to which you have been called, with all humility and gentleness, with patience, bearing with one another in love, making every effort to maintain the unity of the Spirit in the bond of peace.
                                                        Ephesians 4:1-3

There is one body and one Spirit, just as you were called to the one hope of your calling, one Lord, one faith, one baptism, one God and Creator of all, who is above all and through all and in all.   Ephesians 4:4-6

The gifts Christ gave were that some would be apostles, some prophets, some evangelists, some pastors and teachers, to equip the saints for the work of ministry, for building up the body of Christ, until all of us come to the unity of the faith and of the knowledge of the Son of God.
                                                      Ephesians 4:11-13

Speaking the truth in love, we must grow up in every way into him who is the head, into Christ, from whom the whole body, joined and knit together by every ligament with which it is equipped, as each part is working properly, promotes the body's growth in building itself up in love.   Ephesians 4:15-16

Whoever loves a brother or sister lives in the light, but whoever hates another believer is in the darkness, walks in the darkness, and does not know the way to go.
                                                         1 John 2:10-11

Happy are those whom you choose and bring near to live in your courts.

We shall be satisfied with the goodness of your house, your holy temple.

By awesome deeds you answer us with deliverance, O God of our salvation;

You are the hope of all the ends of the earth and of the farthest seas.

By your strength you established the mountains; you are girded with might.

You silence the roaring of the seas, the roaring of their waves, the tumult of the peoples.

Those who live at earth's farthest bounds are awed by your signs;

You make the gateways of the morning and the evening shout for joy.   Psalm 65:4-8

Beloved, let us love one another, because love is from God; everyone who loves is born of God and knows God.

Whoever does not love does not know God, for God is love.

God's love was revealed among us in this way: God sent Christ into the world so that we might live through him.

In this is love, not that we loved God but that God loved us and sent Christ to be the atoning sacrifice for our sins.

Beloved, let us love one another, because love is from God; everyone who loves is born of God. No one has ever seen God;

But if we love one another, God lives in us, and God's love is perfected in us.   1 John 4:7-12

Scripture Selections

Psalm 67; 96; 133. Isaiah 26:12-19; 65:17-25. Jeremiah 31:31-34. Joel 2:23-29. Matthew 16:13-20. John 10:11-16; 15:1-12; 17:18-26. Romans 12. 1 Corinthians 12. Colossians 1; 3:1-17. 1 John 4. Revelation 1:8,12-20.

Prayers

On this day we commend to you, O God, the whole Christian church throughout the world. Bless all who wait upon the name of our Lord Jesus Christ, that they may find strength in their calling. May your grace fill every person, so that those who know your Holy Spirit may ever love your name. Look in mercy at the many wrongs that your church has committed, and be gracious in your judgment. If it be pleasing in your sight, heal the outward divisions of your people. Lead your church, that the world may know your kingdom is truly at hand. This we ask through Jesus Christ. **Amen.**

God of all, who has called us to be your people, we rejoice that on this day the unity of your church is being shown as the faithful throughout the whole earth sit at the Lord's Table and partake of this holy meal. We pray that the faith and witness of all Christian people may increase, and that every wall that still separates them one from another and brings disunity to your church on earth may be broken down; through Jesus Christ. **Amen.**

Let us now strive to walk worthy of the task to which we have been called, with all humility and meekness, with patience, bearing with one another in love, careful to preserve the unity of the Spirit in the bond of peace; one body

and one spirit; even as we have been called in one hope of
our calling; one Lord, one faith, one baptism; one God and
Creator who is above all, and throughout all, and in us all.
Amen.   Ephesians 4:1-6

O Christ, may all that is part of today's encounter be born
of the Spirit of truth and be made fruitful through love.
Behold before us: the past and the future. Behold before
us: the desires of so many hearts. You, who are the God of
history and the God of human hearts, be with us. Christ
Jesus, eternal Son of God, be with us. **Amen.**

Pope John Paul II, 1920–

Blest be the tie that binds
Our hearts in Christian love;
The fellowship of kindred minds
Is like to that above.
    Before the throne of God
    We pour our ardent prayers;
    Our fears, our hopes, our aims, are one,
    Our comforts and our cares. Amen.

John Fawcett, 1740–1817; adapted

May the Holy Spirit guide our prayer toward Jesus Christ
and God the Creator:
Beyond the frontiers of language, race, and nation,
    Unite us, O Jesus.
Beyond our ignorance, our prejudices, and our hostilities,
    Unite us, O Jesus.
Beyond our intellectual and spiritual barriers,
    Unite us, O Jesus.
O God, that goodness and truth may prevail,
    Gather together all Christians.

O God, that there may be only one flock and one shepherd,
Gather together all Christians.
O God, that human pride may be confounded,
Gather together all Christians.
O God, that peace may at last reign on earth,
Gather together all Christians. Amen.

The cup of blessing that we bless, is it not a participation in the blood of Christ? The bread that we break, is it not a participation in the body of Christ? Because there is one loaf, we who are many are one body, for we all partake of the same loaf. As this bread was once scattered upon the mountains, and has now been gathered into one, so may your church be gathered into the unity of your kingdom. All glory be to you, O God, forever and ever!
Gather your church, O God, from the four winds into the kingdom of your love.
Have mercy, O God, on your church; deliver it from all evil, and perfect it in your love. Bring it out of the nations into that unity you have prepared,
Gather your church, O God, from the four winds into the kingdom of your love.
Come, Jesus, come!
Glory be to God forever and ever.
Gather your church, O God, from the four winds into the kingdom of your love. Amen.

Hope for the World

Sentences

God is a stronghold for the oppressed, a stronghold in times of trouble. And those who know your name put their

trust in you, for you, O God, have not forsaken those who
seek you.   Psalm 9:9-10

O God, you will hear the desire of the meek; you will
strengthen their heart, you will incline your ear to do justice for the orphan and the oppressed, so that those from
earth may strike terror no more.   Psalm 10:17-18

When the righteous cry for help, God hears, and rescues
them from all their troubles. God is near to the brokenhearted, and saves the crushed in spirit.   Psalm 34:17-18

May all who seek you rejoice and be glad in you; may
those who love your salvation say continually, "Great is
God!" As for me, I am poor and needy, but God takes
thought for me. You are my help and my deliverer; do not
delay, O my God.   Psalm 40:16-17

Come, behold the works of God; see what desolations God
has brought on the earth. God makes wars cease to the end
of the earth, breaking the bow and shattering the spear.
"Be still, and know that I am God. I am exalted among the
nations."   Psalm 46:8-10

Let justice roll down like waters, and righteousness like an
everflowing stream.   Amos 5:24

God has told you, O mortal, what is good; and what does
God require of you but to do justice, and to love kindness,
and to walk humbly with your God?   Micah 6:8

Blessed are the poor in spirit, for theirs is the kingdom of
   heaven.
Blessed are those who mourn, for they will be comforted.
Blessed are the meek, for they will inherit the earth.

Blessed are those who hunger and thirst for righteousness, for they will be filled.

Blessed are the merciful, for they will receive mercy.

Blessed are the pure in heart, for they will see God.

Blessed are the peacemakers, for they will be called the children of God.   Matthew 5:3-9

Jesus said: "You are the light of the world. Let your light shine before others, so that they may see your good works and give glory to God in heaven."   Matthew 5:14,16

We will praise the name of God with a song; we will magnify God with thanksgiving.

Let the oppressed see it and be glad; you who seek God, let your hearts revive.

For God hears the needy, and does not despise God's own that are in bonds.

Let heaven and earth praise God, the seas and everything that moves in them.

For God will save Zion and rebuild the cities of Judah; and God's servants shall live there and possess it;

The children of God's servants shall inherit it, and those who love God's name shall live in it.

Psalm 69:30-36

Happy are those whose help is the God of Jacob, whose help is in their God,

Who made heaven and earth, the sea, and all that is in them; who keeps faith forever;

Who executes justice for the oppressed; who gives food to the hungry.

God sets the prisoners free; God opens the eyes of the blind. God lifts up those who are bowed down.

God watches over the strangers; God upholds the orphan and the widow, but the way of the wicked God brings to ruin.

God will reign forever, your God, O Zion, for all generations. Psalm 146:5-10

In the days to come the mountain of God's house shall be established as the highest of the mountains, and shall be raised above the hills; all the nations shall stream to it.

Many peoples shall come and say, "Come, let us go up to the mountain of God, to the house of the God of Jacob; that we may be taught God's ways and that we may walk in God's paths."

God shall judge between the nations and shall arbitrate for many peoples; they shall beat their swords into plowshares, and their spears into pruning hooks;

Nation shall not lift sword against nation, neither shall they learn war any more. O house of Jacob, come, let us walk in the light of God! Isaiah 2:2-5

The spirit of God is upon me, and has anointed me; God has sent me to bring good news to the oppressed, to bind up the brokenhearted,

To proclaim liberty to the captives, and release to the prisoners;

To proclaim the year of God's favor, and the day of vengeance of our God; to comfort all who mourn.

For as the earth brings forth its shoots, and as a garden causes what is sown in it to spring up, so God will cause righteousness and praise to spring up before all the nations. Isaiah 61:1-2,11

Scripture Selections

Psalm 2; 8; 9; 24; 31:14-24; 33; 37; 41; 46; 67; 72; 85; 96; 98; Isaiah 11:1-10. Micah 4. Matthew 24:1-14. Acts 17:22-31. Romans 13. Revelation 22:1-5.

Prayers

O Great Spirit, whose voice we hear in the winds and the sea and the cloud, and whose power gives life to all the world: Hear us! We are among your many children. We see with humility and gratefulness your everlasting grace and love. We pray that with strength we may understand the mysteries you have hidden in every leaf and rock. Our wish is not to be superior to our brothers and sisters but to purify our hearts and minds, so that when life fades, as the sunset fades, we may come to you with clean hands and a grateful heart. **Amen.**

Traditional Native American prayer, adapted

We ask you, God, to help and defend us. Deliver the oppressed, pity the insignificant, raise the fallen, show yourself to the needy, heal the sick, bring back those of your people who have gone astray, feed the hungry, lift up the weak, take off the prisoners' chains. May every nation come to know that you alone are God, that Jesus Christ is your child, that we are your people, the sheep that you pasture. **Amen.**   Clement of Rome, c.100

O God, early in the morning I cry to you.
Help me to pray
And to concentrate my thoughts on you:
I cannot do this alone.
In me there is darkness,
But with you there is light;
I am lonely, but you do not leave me;
I am feeble in heart, but with you there is help;
I am restless, but with you there is peace.
In me there is bitterness, but with you there is patience;
I do not understand your ways

But you know the way for me. . . .
Restore me to liberty,
And enable me so to live now
That I may answer before you and before me.
Lord, whatever this day may bring,
Your name be praised.

> Dietrich Bonhoeffer, 1906–1945; from prison

May we be no one's enemy, and may we be the friend of that which is eternal and abides.

May we never quarrel with those nearest us; and if we do, may we be reconciled quickly.

May we love, seek, and attain only that which is good.

May we wish for everyone's happiness and envy none.

May we never rejoice in the ill-fortune of one who has wronged us.

May we win no victory that harms either us or our opponents.

May we reconcile friends who are angry with one another.

May we, to the extent of our power, give all needful help to our friends and all who are in want.

May we never fail a friend who is in danger.

May we respect ourselves. Amen.

> Eusebius of Caesarea, c.340; adapted

Do not fear, for I have redeemed you; I have called you by name, you are mine. When you pass through the waters, I will be with you, they shall not overwhelm you. When you walk through fire you shall not be burned, the flame shall not consume you.

There is a balm in Gilead, to make the wounded whole.

Do not fear, for I am with you; I will bring your offspring from the east, and from the west I will gather you; everyone who is called by my name.

There is a balm in Gilead, to make the wounded whole.

Bring forth the people who are blind, yet have eyes, who are deaf, yet have ears! Let all the nations gather together, and let the peoples assemble. I am about to do a new thing. I will make a way in the wilderness and rivers in the desert.

There is a balm in Gilead, to make the wounded whole.

For I give water in the wilderness to give drink to my chosen people, the people whom I formed for myself so that they might declare my praise.

Everlasting God, revive our souls, that we might drink from your spring and overcome discouragement; that we may praise your mighty acts. We are called by you, to do a new work in your name. Amen.   Isaiah 43 and an African American spiritual

God, make us instruments of your peace.
Where there is hatred, let us sow love,
   Where there is injury, pardon;
Where there is doubt, faith;
   Where there is despair, hope;
Where there is darkness, light;
   Where there is sadness, joy.
O divine Master, grant that we may not so much seek to be consoled, as to console,
   To be understood, as to understand,
To be loved, as to love,
   For it is in giving that we receive;

It is in pardoning that we are pardoned;
It is in dying that we are born to eternal life. Amen.
Francis of Assisi, 1181–1226; adapted

In Christ there is no East or West,
In Christ no South or North;
But one great family of love
Throughout the whole wide earth.
In Christ shall true hearts everywhere
Their high communion find;
His service is the golden chord
Close-binding humankind. Amen.
John Oxenham, 1852–1941; adapted

Reformation Day

Sentences

Your word is a lamp to our feet and a light to our path.
Accept our offerings of praise, O God, and teach us your
ordinances. The wicked have laid a snare for me, but I do
not stray from your precepts. Your decrees are our heritage
forever; they are the joy of our hearts.
Psalm 119:105,108,111

But now, apart from law, the righteousness of God has
been disclosed, and is attested by the law and the prophets, the righteousness of God through faith in Jesus Christ
for all who believe. For there is no distinction, since all
have sinned and fall short of the glory of God; they are
now justified by God's grace as a gift, through the redemption that is in Christ Jesus. Romans 3:21-24

No one can lay any foundation other than the one that has been laid; that foundation is Jesus Christ. Do you not know that you are God's temple and that God's Spirit dwells in you? If anyone destroys God's temple, God will destroy that person. For God's temple is holy, and you are that temple.   1 Corinthians 3:11,16-17

God is our refuge and strength, a very present help in trouble.

Therefore we will not fear, though the earth should change, though the mountains shake in the heart of the sea.

There is a river whose streams make glad the city of God, the holy habitation of the Most High.

God is in the midst of the city; it shall not be moved; God will help it when the morning dawns.

Come, behold the works of God; see what desolations have been brought on the earth. God makes wars to cease to the ends of the earth, breaking the bow and shattering the spear.

The Lord of hosts is with us; the God of Jacob is our refuge.

"Be still, and know that I am God! I am exalted among the nations, I am exalted in the earth."

The Lord of hosts is with us; the God of Jacob is our refuge.   Psalm 46

Let us hear what God will speak, for God will speak peace to the people of faith, those who have turned their hearts to God.

Surely salvation is at hand for those who fear God, that God's glory may dwell in our land.

Steadfast love and faithfulness will meet; righteousness and peace will kiss each other.

The Lord will give what is good, and our land will yield its increase. Righteousness will go before, making a path for God's steps.   Psalm 85:8-10,12-13

Scripture Selections

Psalm 48; 62; 73; 97; 124; 125. Isaiah 55:1-11. Jeremiah 31:31-34. Matthew 12:33-37. John 1:1-5; 8:31-36. Romans 5; 8. Galatians 2:15-21.

Prayers

We thank you, our heavenly Creator, through Jesus Christ your dear child, that you have kept us from all harm and danger; and we pray that you would keep us this day from sin and every evil, that all we do and all we are may please you. Into your hands we commend ourselves, body and soul and all things. Let your holy angels be with us, that the forces of evil may have no power over us. **Amen.**

Based on a prayer by Martin Luther

Our God, who has brought us into fellowship with one another through Jesus Christ: grant us grace and mercy to continue in this ministry together. Help us to do your will when other ways seem easier. Direct our thoughts to you through the reading and preaching of Holy Scripture, that we may always stand in the light of Christ. Bless us in our weakness, O God, that we may better love and serve one another. Make holy our willingness to be obedient to you. We ask this in the name of Christ. **Amen.**

Preserve your word and preaching,
The truth that makes us whole,
The mirror of your glory,
The power that saves the soul.

Oh, may this living water,
This dew of heavenly grace,
Sustain us while here living
Until we see your face. Amen.

Andreas Gryphius, c.1676

Thanksgiving and Harvest

Sentences

You crown the year with your bounty; your wagon tracks overflow with richness. The pastures of the wilderness overflow, the hills gird themselves with joy, the meadows clothe themselves with flocks, the valleys deck themselves with grain, they shout and sing together for joy.

Psalm 65:11-13

It is good to give thanks to God, to sing praises to your name, O Most High; to declare your steadfast love in the morning, and your faithfulness by night, to the music of the lute and the harp, to the melody of the lyre. For you, O God, have made us glad by your work; at the works of your hands we sing for joy.   Psalm 92:1-4

Praise God! O give thanks to God, for God is good, with steadfast love that endures forever!   Psalm 106:1

The eyes of all look to you, and you give them their food in due season. You open your hand, satisfying the desire of every living thing. God is just in all ways, and kind in all doings. God is near to all who call, to all who call in truth.

Psalm 145:15-18

O the depth of the riches and wisdom and knowledge of God! How unsearchable are God's judgments and how inscrutable God's ways! For who has known the mind of God? Or who has been God's counselor? Or who has given a gift to God to receive a gift in return? For from God and through God and to God are all things. To God be the glory forever. Romans 11:33-36

The point is this: the one who sows sparingly will also reap sparingly, and the one who sows bountifully will also reap bountifully. And God is able to provide you with every blessing in abundance, so that by always having enough of everything, you may share abundantly in every good work. 2 Corinthians 9:6,8

God, who supplies seed to the sower and bread for food, will supply and multiply your seed for sowing and increase the harvest of your righteousness. Thanks be to God for this inexpressible gift! 2 Corinthians 9:10,15

Clap your hands, all you peoples; shout to God with loud songs of joy.
For God, the Most High, is awesome, a great king over all the earth.
God has gone up with a shout, the Lord with the sound of a trumpet.
Sing praises to God, sing praises to our King.
Psalm 47:1-2,5-6

May God be gracious to us and bless us and may God's face shine upon us, that your way may be known upon earth, your saving power among all nations.
Let the peoples praise you, O God; let all the peoples praise you.

Let the nations be glad and sing for joy, for you judge the peoples with equity and guide the nations upon earth.

Let the peoples praise you, O God; let all the peoples praise you.

The earth has yielded its increase; God, our God, has blessed us.

May God continue to bless us; let all the ends of the earth revere God. Psalm 67

O come, let us sing to God; let us make a joyful noise to the rock of our salvation!

Let us come into God's presence with thanksgiving; let us make a joyful noise with songs of praise!

For God is a great God, and a great King above all gods.

In God's hands are the deep places of the earth, as well as the heights of the mountains.

The sea is God's, for God made it, and the dry land was formed by God's hands.

O come, let us worship and bow down,

Let us kneel before God, our Maker!

For God is our Creator, and we are the people of God's pasture, the sheep of God's hand.

Psalm 95:1-7

Scripture Selections

Deuteronomy 8:11-20; 16:9-17; 26:1-11; 28:1-14. Psalm 36:5-9; 65; 67; 96; 103; 104; 126; 145; 147; 150. Matthew 13:1-43. Mark 4:1-34. Luke 12:15-34; 17:5-21. 2 Corinthians 8:1-15; 9:6-15. Galatians 5:16–6:10. Revelation 14:13-20.

Prayers

Our God, giver of bounty fully evident in this harvest time, we know that we are not worthy of all your gifts. Yet, out of your great love and mercy you not only have bestowed this material abundance, but beyond all our deserving have given to us a Savior, Jesus Christ. Help us to believe; and in believing, help us to accept; and in accepting, help us to live, that your will, not ours, be done. **Amen.**

To you, O God, do we give our thanks: for your great mercy toward us; for our creation, preservation, and redemption; for the pardon of sin; for the numerous gifts of your love; and for the promise of eternal life in Jesus Christ our Savior. These are your great mercies, but as we rejoice in them we would not forget that you have given us even more. In the ripening of the grain, in the coming to maturity of the fruit, in the abundance which the land so freely yields, we see your hand and we give you our thanks. Enlarge our spirit of thankfulness, that we may with full willingness and in your spirit of giving share our abundance with all who are in need, that they too may praise you; through Jesus Christ. **Amen.**

Creator of heaven and earth, you have studded the sky with stars and made it bright with lights, enriched the earth with fruits to satisfy our needs, given to humankind the clear light and the shining stars to enjoy, the earth's produce to feed on. We pray you, send us rain, abundant, plentiful, fertilizing; and make the earth yield fruit and to spare; for we know how you love us, we know your kindness. Hear our petitions and prayers and bless the whole earth, through Jesus Christ. May glory and power be yours, in the Holy Spirit, now and age after age. **Amen.** Serapion of Thmuis, c.339

Eternal Spirit, the source of all being, the ground of every hope, we gather on this day which is dedicated to gratitude, to offer our thanks to you.

For lives that have been given opportunity to accomplish spiritual tasks in a material world; for tools to labor at these tasks; for abilities and interests; for courage and patience,

We thank you, most gracious God.

For our inner spirit; for peace gained in companionship with you; for all the spirit can do in solitude when left alone in a quiet hour of tranquility with you,

We thank you, most gracious God.

For the fellowship and remembrance of friends; for their faces and names, and the recall of the joy and light they have brought to our lives as they with us have surmounted discouragement, confusion, bewilderment, and loneliness,

We thank you, most gracious God.

For those great souls through whom you have blessed the world: prophets, martyrs, apostles, producers of beauty, those who manifest goodness and truth, who have become our friends as we have lived through their lives and the works they have produced,

We thank you, most gracious God.

For the call to join the family of humankind in building a world where Christ's will rules, where you are called our Creator, and where all men and women are brothers and sisters,

We thank you, most gracious God. Amen.

God and Creator, our hearts are filled with joy and thankfulness to you on this day of festival. Unfailingly, year by year, you clothe the earth in radiant beauty and bid it bring forth its bounteous blessings.

O God, we worship you, our hearts sing your praises.
In humble acknowledgement of your boundless providence, our ancestors brought to your altars on this day the first fruits of their harvest. They chanted songs of gratitude to you for the many gifts of garden and field and for the ripening of the fruit of the spirit.

O God, we worship you, our hearts sing your praises.
Each year at this time your sons and daughters stand before you, celebrating this season and their covenant with you. Let us heed your words of wisdom and do your works of mercy.

O God, we worship you, our hearts sing your praises.
Sanctify us all for your service. Grant that the good seed we sow may ripen into a harvest of righteousness and truth.

O God, we worship you, our hearts sing your praises. Amen.

Union Prayer Book for Jewish Worship, adapted

Praise to God, immortal praise,
For the love that crowns our days;
Bounteous Source of every joy,
Let your praise our tongues employ.
   All to you, our God, we owe,
   Source whence all our blessings flow.
As your prospering hand has blessed,
May we give you of our best
And by deeds of kindly love
For your mercies grateful prove,
   Singing thus through all our days
   Praise to God, immortal praise. Amen.

Anna L. Barbauld, 1743–1825; adapted

Part 5

Special Services

While the services for the Lord's Day provide the basic patterns for worship, there are occasions in the life of the congregation that call for special services. Most of these services can find their place in *The Service for the Lord's Day* at the time of the offertory as an act of dedication. Yet some, such as ordination, marriage, and memorials, are often held apart from the regular worship of the church. We are, therefore, providing for complete services in those special cases.

Baptism of Believers

Baptism should be a part of *The Service for the Lord's Day* and administered in the presence of the whole congregation. Since baptism is an act of dedication, it should rightly come at the time of the offertory. If possible, baptism should be followed by the laying of hands on those baptized, their reception into church membership, and the Lord's Supper. If the Lord's Supper comes at another service, the laying on of hands and the reception into church membership should come at that time.

The minister enters the water and may read one or more of the following Scripture passages, or some other suitable readings:

Then Jesus came from Galilee to John at the Jordan, to be baptized by him. John would have prevented him, saying, "I need to be baptized by you, and do you come to me?" But Jesus answered him, "Let it be so now; for it is proper for us in this way to fulfill all righteousness." Then John consented. And when Jesus had been baptized, just as he came up from the water, suddenly the heavens were opened to him and he saw the Spirit of God descending like a dove and alighting on him. And a voice from heaven said, "This is my Son, the Beloved, with whom I am well pleased."   Matthew 3:13-17

Now when all the people were baptized, and when Jesus also had been baptized and was praying, the heaven was opened, and the Holy Spirit descended upon him in bodily form like a dove. And a voice came from heaven, "You are my Son, the Beloved; with you I am well pleased."
                                                    Luke 3:21-22

Jesus said, "Very truly, I tell you, no one can enter the kingdom of God without being born of water and Spirit. What is born of the flesh is flesh, and what is born of the Spirit is spirit."   John 3:5-6

When the people heard Peter's message, they were cut to the heart and said to Peter and to the other apostles, "Brothers, what shall we do?" Peter said to them, "Repent, and be baptized every one of you in the name of Jesus Christ so that your sins may be forgiven; and you will receive the gift of the Holy Spirit." So those who welcomed the message were baptized, and that day about three thousand persons were added. They devoted themselves to the apostles' teaching and fellowship, to the breaking of bread and the prayers.　　Acts 2:37-38,41-42

And now why do you delay? Get up, be baptized, and have your sins washed away, calling on Jesus' name. Acts 22:16

Do you not know that all of us who have been baptized into Christ Jesus were baptized into his death? Therefore we have been buried with him by baptism into death, so that, just as Christ was raised from the dead by the glory of God, so we too might walk in newness of life.

Romans 6:3-4

If you confess with your lips that Jesus is Lord and believe in your heart that God raised him from the dead, you will be saved. For one believes with the heart and so is justified, and one confesses with the mouth and so is saved. The scripture says, "No one who believes in him will be put to shame."　　Romans 10:9-11

Just as the body is one and has many members, and all the members of the body, though many, are one body, so it is with Christ. For in the one Spirit we were all baptized into one body—Jews or Greeks, slaves or free—and we were all made to drink of one Spirit.　　1 Corinthians 12:12-13

In Christ you are all children of God through faith. As many of you as were baptized into Christ have clothed yourselves with Christ. There is no longer Jew or Greek, there is no longer slave or free, there is no longer male and female, for all of you are one in Christ Jesus.

Galatians 3:26-28

When you were buried with Christ in baptism, you were also raised with him through faith in the power of God, who raised him from the dead. Colossians 2:12

Fight the good fight of the faith; take hold of the eternal life to which you were called when you made the good confession in the presence of many witnesses. 1 Timothy 6:12

Baptism now saves you—not as a removal of dirt from the body, but as an appeal to God for a good conscience, through the resurrection of Jesus Christ, who has gone into heaven and is at the right hand of God, with angels, authorities, and powers made subject to him. 1 Peter 3:21-22

Those to be baptized enter the water and the minister says:
Hear these words of Jesus: "All authority in heaven and on earth has been given to me. Go therefore and make disciples of all nations, baptizing them in the name of the Father and of the Son and of the Holy Spirit, and teaching them to obey everything that I have commanded you. And remember, I am with you always, to the end of the age."
Matthew 28:18-20

The minister, using his or her own words or the following, addresses the congregation and those who are to be baptized:
Baptism is one of the two sacraments (*ordinances*) given by Christ to his followers. In baptism, through faith we are made one with Christ. We are buried with Christ and with him raised from the dead to walk in new life. The washing of our bodies with water is the outward and visible sign of the cleansing of our inner being through the grace of our Savior Jesus Christ. We are baptized not only with water but also with the Holy Spirit, and by this same Spirit we

are baptized into Christ's body, the church, and made members of the whole people of God.

In obedience to Christ's command let us baptize these who have professed their faith in him.

The minister, stating the name of each person to be baptized, addresses each one with these words:
(Name), do you before God and this congregation affirm through this act of baptism your faith in Christ as your Lord and Savior, and do you promise to follow Christ in word and deed throughout your life?

The person to be baptized answers:
I do.

Those who were baptized as children may desire to receive adult baptism as a confirmation of their personal relationship to and faith in Jesus Christ. For them, baptism becomes an act of personal confession and a confirmation of the baptism which was given to them as children and the promises made on their behalf by parents and godparents. The following words may be used:
(Name), do you now confirm the vows taken by your parents on your behalf in infancy? Do you believe in God as your eternal Father, in Jesus Christ as your Savior and Lord, and in the Holy Spirit as your comforter?

The person to be baptized answers:
I do.

The minister says:
Let us pray.
Loving God, may your Spirit fall upon *(Name)* and remain with *him/her* all the days of *his/her* life. And may the joy of this moment be *his/hers* forever. **Amen.**

The minister then says:
Upon the declaration of your faith and in obedience to Christ's command, on behalf of this congregation I baptize you, *(Full Name),* in the name of God: Father, Son, and Holy Spirit. **Amen.**

The minister then baptizes each candidate. After all have been baptized, the minister says:
We have done as Christ has commanded. As those who have been baptized have confessed their faith and committed themselves to discipleship, let us all renew our baptismal vows as we pray:
Gracious God, baptize us afresh with your Spirit. May we know once again the newness of life so abundantly shown to these who have been baptized. Open our hearts to receive them into our midst, that they may know among us the same spirit of love that was in Christ, who loved us and gave himself for us. **Amen.**

Other Scripture Selections

Mark 1:1-13. Acts 8:36-40; 9:1-19; 10:34-38; 16:11-15; 16:16-34; 19:1-7. Ephesians 4:1-6; 5:21-33. Colossians 3:1-17. Titus 3:4-7. Hebrews 10:19-25. 1 John 5:6-12.

Alternate Prayers

Almighty and everlasting God, we give you humble and hearty thanks for our Savior Jesus Christ, who died for our sins, was buried, and was raised. Graciously accept these your servants, that they, coming to you in baptism, may be united with Christ in his church, and receive according to your promise the forgiveness of their sins and the gift of the Holy Spirit. Grant that they, putting on the Lord Jesus Christ, may receive of his fullness and always abide in him. Keep them strong in faith, steadfast in hope, abounding in love. Bestow upon them the many gifts of your grace, that they may serve you well in your church. Defend them in all trials and temptations, and grant that, enduring to the end, they may inherit eternal life; through Jesus Christ our Lord. **Amen.**

Send your blessing, we ask you, O Lord, upon these your servants, who today acknowledge before all their desire to be disciples of Jesus Christ. Strengthen them by your Spirit, that they may lead lives worthy of the confession they have made. Teach them to serve you with loyal and steadfast hearts; to give and not to count the cost; to fight and not to heed the wounds; to strive and not to seek for rest; to labor and to ask for no reward, save that of knowing that they do your will; through Jesus Christ our Lord. **Amen.**

Grant, O Lord, that these who have in baptism made public confession of the lordship of Jesus Christ may in their lives in the world continually show that they are his disciples. Through their witness may others come to believe in him whom to know is life eternal, Christ our Lord. **Amen.**

May we, O Lord, in witnessing anew the coming of these baptized to you, renew our covenant with you, that we may continue to walk in newness of life; through the grace of our Lord Jesus Christ. **Amen.**

We thank you, our Creator, for every renewal which comes in life. May this baptism be for these who are to be baptized a springtime that will prepare them for a summer of growth and an autumn of abundant harvest. Plant within them the seeds of your Spirit that their lives may bear richly the fruits of that same Spirit; through Jesus Christ our Lord. **Amen.**

Commissioning of Those Who Have Been Baptized

A service of commissioning follows baptism, and will usually take place before the Lord's Supper. Such a service was practiced in ancient times, as well as by the General Baptists of Great Britain. Its basic intent is confirmation of the faith that has been expressed in baptism and the commissioning of those baptized to their ministry in the church and world.

The minister says:
Following an ancient practice of the church, we are now to commission those who have been baptized to ministry as priests and servants of Jesus Christ by the laying on of hands and prayer. Let us as members of this congregation join with them and renew our commitment to the servant ministry of Christ. Let us now, with them, hear the words of Scripture.

The minister or a lay worship leader reads one or more of the following Scripture passages:
You are a chosen race, a royal priesthood, a holy nation, God's own people, in order that you may proclaim the mighty acts of the one who called you out of darkness into light.   1 Peter 2:9

Above all, maintain constant love for one another. Be hospitable to one another without complaining. Like good stewards of the manifold grace of God, serve one another with whatever gift each of you has received. Whoever speaks must do so as one speaking the very words of God; whoever serves must do so with the strength that God supplies, so that God may be glorified in all things through Jesus Christ. To him belong the glory and the power forever and ever. Amen.   1 Peter 4:8-11

Love one another with mutual affection; outdo one another in showing honor. Do not lag in zeal, be ardent in spirit, serve the Lord. Rejoice in hope, be patient in suffering, persevere in prayer. Contribute to the needs of the saints; extend hospitality to strangers.   Romans 12:10-13

Jesus said, "You are the light of the world. Let your light shine before others, so that they may see your good works and give glory to God in heaven."   Matthew 5:14,16

Jesus said, "I give you a new commandment, that you love one another. Just as I have loved you, you also should love one another."   John 13:34

Those who have been baptized kneel before the table and the minister prays extempore or as follows:
Eternal God, cause your Spirit to come upon these your servants to empower them for your ministry in the church and in the world. May they be so filled with your love that, as they live in the world, the world may come to know through them the love of Christ. In all their ministry help them truly to serve you and give you the glory. **Amen.**

The minister and one or two lay members shall place their hands in turn on the head of each one who has been baptized and the minister shall pray:
Bless, O God, this your servant and empower *him/her* by your Holy Spirit to be a faithful minister of Jesus Christ our Lord. **Amen.**

The newly commissioned ones stand and the minister says:
You are no longer strangers and aliens, but you are members of the household of God. On behalf of this congregation I welcome you. The peace of God go with you and remain with you always. **Amen.**

The Lord's Supper may follow, with the newly baptized receiving Communion for the first time as members of the church.

Dedication of a Child

The dedication service should be a part of a regular worship service of the church. It may be included in the offertory, as an act signifying the offering of the child to God. As the gifts are brought forward a representative of the congregation escorts the parents and the child to a place before the table. (This service may be adapted for a single parent.)

After the dedication of the gifts the minister says:
We welcome *(Names of Parents)*, who have brought their child *(Name)* to be dedicated to God, the maker of all things and the giver of life. In doing so we follow the way of Jesus who said, "Let the little children come to me; for it is to such as these that the kingdom of God belongs."

The minister, addressing the parents, says:
In presenting *(Name)* to God, do you promise that through the grace given you and in partnership with the congregation you will teach *him/her* the truths and responsibilities of the Christian faith, and seek to lead *him/her* into a living relationship with Jesus Christ?

The parents reply:
We will.

The minister addresses the congregation, saying:
Do you, the members of this congregation, accept the responsibility, together with the parents, to teach this child, that *he/she* may be brought to full maturity in Jesus Christ? If so, will you signify your acceptance by standing?

As the congregation stands, the minister takes the child into his or her arms and gives a blessing:
(Name), God bless you and keep you. God's face shine upon you and be gracious to you. God look upon you with favor and give you peace. **Amen.**

The minister returns the child to the parents, and then says:
Let us pray.
Even as Mary and Joseph brought the child Jesus to your house that he might be consecrated to your service, so these parents have brought this little one to this place, that among your people they might present *him/her* to you. Give to these parents your special graces of insight and love, that under their guidance *(Name)* may grow in wisdom and stature and in favor with you and all people. Grant that we your people may truly be a household of faith to *(Name),* providing *him/her* with food for the spirit to nourish *him/her* through the years of growth into maturity. With gratitude to

you for this child we dedicate *him/her, his/her* parents, and ourselves, to the end that *his/her* life may be a blessing to you and a service to humanity. **Amen.**

Here the minister may present a certificate of dedication to the parents. The worship service then continues.

Reception of Church Members

The reception of new members of the congregation should take place in *The Service for the Lord's Day* as part of the offertory.

As the gifts are brought to the table the new members come forward. After the dedication of the gifts, the minister, addressing the congregation, says:
We welcome in the name of Jesus Christ these who have come to join in the life and ministry of this congregation. As you receive them, do you promise before God and in their presence to give them your love and encouragement as they grow in their Christian life and commitment?

The congregation shall answer:
We do.

The minister may read one or more of the following Scripture passages and say some words concerning the meaning and responsibilities of church membership.
As in one body we have many members, and not all the members have the same function, so we, who are many, are one body in Christ and individually we are members of one another. We have gifts that differ according to the grace given to us.   Romans 12:4-6

Let love be genuine; hate what is evil, hold fast to what is good; love one another with mutual affection; outdo one another in showing honor. Do not lag in zeal, be ardent in spirit, serve the Lord. Rejoice in hope, be patient in suffering, persevere in prayer. Contribute to the needs of the saints; extend hospitality to strangers.   Romans 12:9-13

The fruit of the Spirit is love, joy, peace, patience, kindness, generosity, faithfulness, gentleness, and self-control. So let us not grow weary in doing what is right. Whenever we have an opportunity, let us work for the good of all, and especially for those of the family of faith.
Galatians 5:22-23; 6:9-10

Lead a life worthy of the calling to which you have been called, with all humility and gentleness, with patience, bearing with one another in love, making every effort to maintain the unity of the Spirit in the bond of peace. There is one body and one Spirit, just as you were called to the one hope of your calling, one Lord, one faith, one baptism, one God and Creator of all, who is above all and through all and in all. Speaking the truth in love, we must grow up in every way into him who is the head, into Christ, from whom the whole body, joined and knit together by every ligament with which it is equipped, as each part is working properly, promotes the body's growth in building itself up in love.   Ephesians 4:1-6,15-16

The minister then addresses each new member by name:
(Name), do you promise to be a faithful follower of Jesus Christ and to serve him gladly in this congregation?

Each person addressed answers:
I do.

Then the minister prays extempore, or as follows:
We thank you, O God, for these who have come to join our family of faith. May they find among us a deep love and concern for them and their well-being. Enable them to find their place of service among us. Grant that they may grow up in every way into him who is the head of the church, Christ Jesus our Lord. **Amen.**

The minister takes in turn the hand of each new member and says:
In the name of Jesus Christ and on behalf of this congregation, I welcome you into the membership of this church and extend to you its hand of fellowship.

A certificate of church membership may then be presented to each new member. A representative of the congregation says:
This certificate indicates that you are a member of this church in good standing with all the rights, privileges, and responsibilities that such membership entails.

After each new member has been welcomed and presented with a certificate, the minister says:
You are no longer strangers and aliens, but you are citizens with the saints and also members of the household of God, built upon the foundation of the apostles and prophets, with Christ Jesus himself as the cornerstone. In him the whole structure is joined together and grows into a temple in the Lord, in whom you also are built together spiritually into a dwelling place for God.   Ephesians 2:19-22

The service then proceeds with the Lord's Supper.

Marriage

Marriage services often need to be adapted to local needs and situations. The following is a suggested guide for a marriage service which is a service of worship. The service may be used alone or included in *The Service for the Lord's Day* at the time of the offertory.

> Prelude
>
> Lighting of the candles
>
> Entrance of family members and participants (with appropriate music)
>
> > Seating of the grandparents (groom's to the right of the center aisle facing the front of the sanctuary, bride's to the left)
> >
> > Seating of the parents (the groom's parents first, seated to the right of the center aisle, followed by the bride's mother, seated on the left of the center aisle)
> >
> > Minister, groom, best man, and groom's attendants enter and take their places on the right, then turn and face the rear of the sanctuary
>
> The bridal procession
>
> > Bride's attendants enter, come down the aisle and take their places on the left, facing the rear of the sanctuary
> >
> > Maid/Matron of honor enters, comes down the aisle and takes her place on the left

Ring bearer and flower girl enter, come down the aisle and take their places, the ring bearer beside the best man and the flower girl beside the maid/matron of honor

Bride enters, accompanied by her father, other relative, or friend, while the congregation stands and remains standing until the wedding party is seated

Statement of purpose by the minister

Invocation

Hymn

Scripture readings

Sermon

Bride, groom, best man, maid/matron of honor, flower girl, and ring bearer take their places in front of the table, facing the minister

Declarations of acceptance, presentations, vows, exchange of rings, prayer, and pronouncement of marriage

Lighting of the unity candle

Family blessing

Pastoral prayer and blessing

Introduction of the newly married couple

The Lord's Supper (if observed)

Recessional (bride and groom, followed by ring bearer and flower girl, maid/matron of honor and best man, bride's and groom's attendants)

Reception

The Marriage Service

After the procession, the minister says:
Dear friends, *(Name)* and *(Name)* have come to offer themselves to God and to each other in the holy bond of marriage. Marriage has been established for human welfare and enjoyment. Marriage makes sacred the bond between two persons and offers to each the opportunity to know more fully the love of God through the love which they share with one another. This union of two persons in body, mind, and spirit is a gift from God and is for their mutual comfort and joy. It is to be entered into reverently and in good faith in accordance with the purposes for which it was instituted by God. It is to this sacred union that *(Name)* and *(Name)* now give themselves to one another, seeking the blessing of God upon their life together.

Let us pray.
God of love, who has brought *(Name)* and *(Name)* to this place to offer themselves to one another in holy marriage, we pray that you will grant them every good and perfect blessing. May their love continue to grow in depth and meaning. Help them to share fully their mutual joys and sorrows and continually to carry one another's loads. Grant that their temptations may be few, and may they always be ready and willing to forgive even as you forgive them. We ask these mercies in the name of Jesus Christ, who has taught us to say when we pray:
Our Father . . .

A hymn is sung, after which the wedding party and congregation are seated. Scripture lessons are read and a sermon is given. After the sermon the minister invites the bride, groom, maid/matron of honor, best man, flower girl, and ring bearer to come and stand before the table. The other attendants may take their assigned places.

The minister says to the man:
(Name), will you have *(Name)* to be your wedded wife, to live together in the holy bond of marriage, to love her, comfort her, honor and keep her; and forsaking all others be faithful to her as long as you both shall live? If so, answer, I will.
The man answers:
   I will.

The minister then says to the woman:
(Name), will you have *(Name)* to be your wedded husband, to live together in the holy bond of marriage, to love him, comfort him, honor and keep him; and forsaking all others be faithful to him as long as you both shall live? If so, answer, I will.
The woman answers:
   I will.

The minister then says:
Who presents *(Name, Woman)* to be married to *(Name, Man)*?
The one(s) making the presentation answer(s) as follows, or use(s) other appropriate words:
   I (we) do.

The minister then says:
Who presents *(Name, Man)* to be married to *(Name, Woman)*?
The one(s) making the presentation answer(s) as follows, or use(s) other appropriate words:
   I (we) do.

The minister then says to the man and woman:
Will you join your right hands for the giving and receiving of the marriage vows?

The man, following the minister, says to the woman:
I, *(Name)*, take you, *(Name)*, to be my wife. I promise before God and these friends to be your loving and faithful husband, to share with you in plenty and in want, in joy and in sorrow, in sickness and in health, and to join with you so that together we may serve God and others, as long as we both shall live.

While their hands are still joined the woman, following the minister, says to the man:
I, *(Name)*, take you, *(Name)*, to be my husband. I promise before God and these friends to be your loving and faithful wife, to share with you in plenty and in want, in joy and in sorrow, in sickness and in health, and to join with you so that together we may serve God and others, as long as we both shall live.

They release their hands. The minister asks for the ring(s) with these words:
What token(s) have you to symbolize the faithful fulfillment of your marriage vows?

The best man takes the ring(s) from the ring bearer and gives them to the minister who says:
This ring is/These rings are the outward and visible symbol of the inward and spiritual bond that unites *(Name)* and *(Name)* in abiding love.

The minister says to the man:
(Name), will you place this ring upon *(Name)*'s finger and say after me:

Name, I give you this ring as a token of the promises made this day between us, and as a pledge of our enduring love. May the God of all love bless you now and forever.

If there is a second ring, the minister gives it to the woman and says:
(Name), will you place this ring upon *(Name)*'s finger and say after me:

Name, I give you this ring as a token of the promises made this day between us, and as a pledge of our enduring love. May the God of all love bless you now and forever.

The minister says:
Let us pray.
Bless, O God, *(Name)* and *(Name)*, that for them *this ring/ these rings* may be a constant reminder of the promises made this day to one another and to you. **Amen.**

The minister then says:
Since *(Name)* and *(Name)* have consented to join together in marriage and have witnessed the same before God and this company, and have pledged their mutual love to each other and have declared the same by the giving and receiving of *a ring/rings* and by joining hands, I declare that they are husband and wife. The God of all love has joined you one to another. Go now in peace, trusting that the love which you now know will forever make you one.

The unity candle may now be lit by the bride and groom, followed by family blessings. If desired, the bride and groom may kneel for the closing prayer and blessing.

The minister says:
Let us pray.
Gracious God, continue to show your love to *(Name)* and *(Name)*, who in the presence of family and friends have given their mutual pledge to live together as husband and wife. Grant them the strength and patience, the affection and understanding, the courage and love to abide in peace according to your will for them. God bless you and keep you. God's face shine upon you and be gracious to you. God look upon you with favor and give you peace. **Amen.**

The minister may then introduce the newly married couple, using the names by which they shall henceforth be known. If the Lord's Supper is to be observed it shall take place at this time. It can follow the order as set forth in The Service for the Lord's Day.

The service concludes with the recessional, after which the members of the congregation may greet the bride and groom.

Blessing of a Civil Marriage

The service may be used alone or included in *The Service for the Lord's Day* as part of the offertory. If used alone, include the items marked by a star(*). The following is a suggested order.

> Statement of purpose by the minister
> Prayer
> *Scripture readings
> *Sermon
> Reaffirmation of promises

Blessing of the marriage symbols and those who wear
  them
Affirmation of the marriage
Prayer and blessing
*Benediction

The Service of Blessing

*The minister states the purpose of the service, using the
following or other words:*
(Name) and *(Name)* have been joined in marriage according to the laws of the state. They now come to declare their
love for one another and to seek and receive the blessing
of God and the church upon their marriage.

The minister says:
Let us pray.
Loving God, we bring before you *(Name)* and *(Name)* who
come seeking your blessing and that of the church as they
confirm their marriage vows. Be with them and make of
this a holy hour filled with your gracious presence. **Amen.**

*If the service is used alone, Scripture readings and the
sermon are included here.*

The minister then addresses the man, saying:
(Name), you have given yourself to *(Name)* to be united
with her in marriage. Do you reaffirm the promises you
have made to love her and keep to her in the holy bond of
marriage, to stand by her side in sickness and in health, in
plenty and in want, in joy and in sorrow, as long as you
both shall live? If so, answer by saying, I do.
The man shall answer:
  I do.

The minister addresses the woman, saying:
(Name), you have given yourself to *(Name)* to be united with him in marriage. Do you reaffirm the promises you have made to love him and keep to him in the holy bond of marriage, to stand by his side in sickness and in health, in plenty and in want, in joy and in sorrow, as long as you both shall live? If so answer by saying, I do.
The woman shall answer:
   I do.

The minister shall place a hand upon the ring(s) and say:
Grant your blessing upon *(Name)* and *(Name)* as they wear *this symbol/these symbols* of the covenant made between them, and may *this ring/these rings* be for them a constant reminder of the perfect love made known in Jesus Christ, in whose name we pray. **Amen.**

The minister then unites the right hands of the man and woman and says:
You have been joined by God. Let no one separate you. *(Name)* and *(Name)*, your marriage has been honored by God and the church. Give yourself unselfishly to one another; be united in love; live in peace. God be with you always.

Let us pray.
Gracious God, continue to show your love to *(Name)* and *(Name)*, who in the presence of family and friends and in the midst of this congregation have reaffirmed their marriage vows and pledged their mutual assent to live together as husband and wife. Grant them the strength and patience, the affection and understanding, the courage and love to abide in unity according to your will for them.

God bless you and keep you. God's face shine upon you and be gracious to you. God look upon you with favor and give you peace. **Amen.**

At the conclusion of the service opportunity may be given for the members of the congregation to give their personal blessings and congratulations to the couple.

Memorial Service

The service is an act of corporate worship celebrating the life of the deceased and offering consolation to the bereaved. It is appropriately held in the place where the congregation regularly gathers. The service includes hymns, prayers, and the reading and proclamation of God's Word. If it is held in a mortuary chapel, it should remain an act of corporate worship and allow for congregational participation in the service.

After a prelude the minister may say one or more of the following:
The eternal God is your dwelling place, and underneath are the everlasting arms.   Deuteronomy 33:27 (RSV)

Weeping may linger for the night, but joy comes in the morning.   Psalm 30:5

God is our refuge and strength, a very present help in trouble.   Psalm 46:1

You, O God, have been our dwelling place in all generations. Before the mountains were brought forth, or ever you had formed the earth and the world, from everlasting to everlasting you are God.   Psalm 90:1-2

Our help is in the name of God, who made heaven and earth.   Psalm 124:8

Do not fear, for I am with you; do not be afraid, for I am your God. I will strengthen you, I will help you, I will uphold you with my victorious hand.   Isaiah 41:10

Blessed are those who mourn, for they will be comforted.
                                                                       Matthew 5:4

Jesus said, "I am the resurrection and the life. Those who believe in me, even though they die, will live, and every-one who lives and believes in me will never die."
                                                                       John 11:25-26

Blessed be the God and Father of our Lord Jesus Christ! By God's great mercy we have been given a new birth into a living hope through the resurrection of Jesus Christ from the dead, and into an inheritance that is imperishable, undefiled, and unfading.   1 Peter 1:3-4

The home of God is among mortals. God will dwell with them and they will be God's peoples. God will wipe every tear from their eyes. Death will be no more; mourning and crying and pain will be no more, for the first things have passed away.   Revelation 21:3-4

A hymn may be sung, after which the minister says:
Lift up your hearts.
   We lift them up to God.
O God, open our lips,
   And our mouth shall show forth your praise.

Let us pray.
Eternal Spirit, before whom the generations rise and pass

away, even in the presence of death our first words to you are in praise for your unnumbered mercies. For the memory of loved ones now departed, we praise you. For their victories of character over trial, of courage over difficulty, of faith over sorrow, we give you thanks, and for all those who have done justly, loved mercy, and walked humbly with their God, we sing joyfully to you. Grant us now this same joyful thanksgiving as we remember our friend, and give to us that sure knowledge that you have won the victory over death in the resurrection of Jesus Christ. **Amen.**

or

Eternal God, in whom we live and move and have our being, and who by your mighty power raised Jesus Christ from the dead, give us the light and life of your presence. Help us to put our trust in your wisdom and to open ourselves to the ministry of your love. Open our hearts, that we may truly hear your words of encouragement as they come to us from the Scriptures, and that by their consolation we may be lifted out of our sorrow to know that in Christ there is life eternal. **Amen.**

Psalm 23 may be read or sung. (Other appropriate psalms are 16, 39, 116, 121, or 130.)

God is my shepherd: I shall not want.

God makes me lie down in green pastures and leads me beside the still waters.

God restores my soul and leads me in right paths.

Even though I walk through the darkest valley, I fear no evil, for you are with me; your rod and your staff, they comfort me.

You prepare a table before me in the presence of my enemies; you anoint my head with oil; my cup overflows.

Surely goodness and mercy shall follow me all the days of my life, and I shall dwell in the house of God my whole life long. Psalm 23, adapted

The minister then says:
We are gathered here to hear God's word of hope as we commemorate with thanksgiving the life of *(Name)*.

It is customary at this point in the service to give a brief biographical statement of the deceased.

Then may be read selections from the following or other suitable passages of Scripture.
Jesus said, "Do not let your hearts be troubled. Believe in God, believe also in me. In God's house there are many dwelling places. If it were not so, would I have told you that I go to prepare a place for you? And if I go and prepare a place for you, I will come again and will take you to myself, so that where I am there you may be also. Peace I leave with you, my peace I give to you. Do not let your hearts be troubled, and do not let them be afraid."
John 14:1-3,27

We know that all things work together for good for those who love God. If God is for us, who is against us? Who will separate us from the love of Christ? Will hardship, or distress, or persecution, or famine, or nakedness, or peril, or sword? No, in all these things we are more than conquerors through him who loved us. For I am convinced that neither death, nor life, nor angels, nor rulers, nor things present, nor things to come, nor powers, nor height, nor depth, nor anything else in all creation, will be able to separate us from the love of God in Christ Jesus our Lord.
Romans 8:28,31,35,37-39

Christ has been raised from the dead, the first fruits of those who have died. For since death came through a human being, the resurrection from the dead has also come through a human being, for as all die in Adam, so all will be made alive in Christ. But someone will ask, "How are the dead raised? With what kind of a body do they come?" Fool! What you sow does not come to life unless it dies. And as for what you sow, you do not sow the body that is to be, but a bare seed, perhaps of wheat or of some other grain. But God gives it a body as God has chosen, and to each kind of seed its own body. So it is with the resurrection of the dead. What is sown is perishable, what is raised is imperishable. It is sown in dishonor, it is raised in glory. It is sown in weakness, it is raised in power. It is sown a physical body, it is raised a spiritual body. Flesh and blood cannot inherit the kingdom of God, nor does the perishable inherit the imperishable. When this perishable body puts on imperishability, then the saying that is written will be fulfilled:

"Death has been swallowed up in victory."
"Where, O death, is your victory?
Where, O death, is your sting?"
Thanks be to God, who gives us the victory through our Lord Jesus Christ.

1 Corinthians 15:20-22,35-38,42-44,50,54-55,57

Do not lose heart. Though our outer nature is wasting away, our inner nature is being renewed day by day. For this slight momentary affliction is preparing us for an eternal weight of glory beyond all measure, because we look not at what can be seen but at what cannot be seen; for what can be seen is temporary, but what cannot be seen is eternal. For we know that if the earthly tent we live in is destroyed, we have a building from God, a house not made with hands, eternal in the heavens. 2 Corinthians 4:16-5:1

May grace and peace be yours in abundance. By God's great mercy we have been given a new birth into a living hope through the resurrection of Jesus Christ from the dead, and into an inheritance that is imperishable, undefiled, and unfading, kept in heaven for you, who are being protected by the power of God through faith for a salvation ready to be revealed in the last time. In this you rejoice.

1 Peter 1:2-6

I saw a new heaven and a new earth, for the first heaven and the first earth had passed away, and the sea was no more. And I saw the holy city, the new Jerusalem, coming down out of heaven from God, prepared as a bride adorned for her husband. And I heard a voice from heaven saying, "See, the home of God is among mortals. God will dwell with them; they will be God's peoples. God will wipe every tear from their eyes. Death will be no more; mourning and crying and pain will be no more, for the first things have passed away." Revelation 21:1-4

The Gloria Patri, *the Doxology, or a hymn of affirmation may be sung, followed by a brief sermon on one of the Scripture texts dealing with the victory of Christ over death and the hope which Christ's victory brings to humankind.*

An appropriate anthem or solo may be presented.

One or more of the following prayers, or an extemporaneous prayer, may then be offered.
God of all grace and glory, who sent Jesus Christ to bring life and immortality to light, we give you thanks that by his

death he destroyed the power of death. By his resurrection he gave assurance that because he lives we too shall live, and that neither death nor life, nor things present nor things to come, shall be able to separate us from your love, which we have seen in Christ Jesus. **Amen.**

Merciful God, comfort us as we face the valley of the shadow of death. Lift our eyes from the dark depths to the hills from whence help comes. Aid us to see your light, that it may be for us a light upon the path and a lamp upon the way until we come into the fullness of your presence, where there is no shadow or hiding. **Amen.**

Eternal God, let your mercy rest upon us as we with grateful affection remember *(Name)*, who has departed this life. We thank you for *his/her* days upon the earth and the joy that *he/she* brought to many. May our remembrance of *him/her* live long among us and be to us a source of guidance and strength. Give to those who miss *him/her* most deeply wells of consolation from which to draw comfort, and enable us to be your ministers of mercy to them in their time of need. **Amen.**

The congregation joins the minister in the Lord's Prayer, after which the minister says:
May the God of peace, who brought back from the dead our Lord Jesus, the great shepherd of the sheep, by the blood of the eternal covenant, make you complete in everything good so that you may live in accord with the divine will, doing that which is pleasing in God's sight, through Jesus Christ, to whom be the glory forever and ever. **Amen.**   Hebrews 13:20-21

or

Go in peace, and may the blessing of God the Creator, Christ the Redeemer, and the Holy Spirit the Comforter be with you, and remain with you now and forever. **Amen.**

The benediction and blessing is followed by a postlude.

Committal Service

The service of committal is generally held at the place of interment of the remains of the deceased. However, the words of committal may be included in the memorial service.

After the people have taken their places, the service begins as the minister says one or more of the following Scripture sentences:
I know that my Redeemer lives, and will stand upon the earth at the last; then I shall see God.   Job 19:25-26

Jesus said, ''I am the resurrection and the life. Those who believe in me, even through they die, will live, and everyone who lives and believes in me will never die.''
                                                    John 11:25-26

''Death has been swallowed up in victory. Where, O death, is your victory? Where, O death, is your sting?'' Thanks be to God, who gives us the victory through our Lord Jesus Christ.   1 Corinthians 15:55,57

The home of God is among mortals. God will dwell with them; they will be God's peoples. God will wipe every tear from their eyes. Death will be no more; mourning and crying and pain will be no more, for the first things have passed away.   Revelation 21:3-4

Then shall be said the words of committal:
Eternal God, whose loving care is over all, we commit the earthly remains of *(Name)* to the *earth/sea/elements,* believing that *his/her* spirit is with you, whom to know is life eternal. **Amen.**

Then shall be said:
I heard a voice from heaven saying: "Write this: Blessed are the dead who from now on die in the Lord." "Yes," says the Spirit, "they will rest from their labors, for their deeds follow them." Revelation 14:13

Let us pray.
Almighty God, who by the death and resurrection of Jesus Christ revealed your victory over sin and death, grant that we may live in the power of that triumph. May we give witness throughout our whole lives to the one who is the resurrection and the life, who lives and reigns with you and the Holy Spirit, world without end. **Amen.**

Let us go forth in the Spirit of Christ, and may God bless you and keep you. God's face shine upon you and be gracious to you. God look upon you with favor and give you peace. **Amen.**

Memorial for a Child

After the playing of a prelude the minister may say one of the following passages from Scripture:
See, God comes. He will feed his flock like a shepherd; he will gather the lambs in his arms, and carry them in his bosom. Isaiah 40:10-11

God says, "As a mother comforts her child, so I will comfort you; you shall be comforted."   Isaiah 66:13

Blessed are those who mourn, for they will be comforted.
                                                    Matthew 5:4

People brought little children to Jesus in order that he might touch them. He said, "Let the little children come to me, for it is to such as these that the kingdom of God belongs." And he took them up in his arms, laid his hands on them, and blessed them.   Mark 10:13-14

The minister then shall say:
Let us pray.
Loving Parent God, we come to you this day, our hearts sorrowful over the loss of your child and ours. We turn to you and give ourselves to your loving care. Speak to us words of consolation and comfort. Lift us out of the darkness of our distress into the light and peace of your presence, and may we go from this place knowing that all things work together for good for those who love you. **Amen.**

Psalm 23 may be said or sung, followed by the reading of one or more Scripture selections. The following or other suitable passages may be read: Matthew 18:1-5; 18:10-14. Mark 10: 13-16. John 14:1-6; 14:18,27. 1 Corinthians 13. Revelation 21:4. Zechariah 8:5.

An address may then be given, followed by a hymn or special music.

The minister then prays extempore, or as follows:
Let us pray.
God of love and mercy, we thank you for *(Name)*, who has

tarried for awhile among us. We have been blessed by *his/her* presence and *he/she* has brought a blessing to those who have been closest to *him/her*. We thank you for the love which *he/she* has called forth and for the memories of *his/her* presence that will continue to bless the family of which *he/she* has been a part. Grant that those who have cared for *him/her* and who have poured out their love upon *him/her* may be deepened in their faith, and that through their sorrow their spirits may be renewed. **Amen.**

Gracious God, who in Jesus Christ promised comfort to those who mourn, be present with these parents who have suffered the loss of their child. Grant that in their sorrow they may be brought closer to you and to each other and that their hearts may be filled with your presence and peace. **Amen.**

Loving Christ, you took little children into your arms and said, ''to such belong the kingdom of God.'' We rest in the assurance that this little one is with you. Strengthen our faith, that we too may believe that all who become like little children are now and evermore with you. **Amen.**

Then the Lord's Prayer may be said, followed by a hymn and the dismissal.

The minister shall say:
Go in peace; and the blessing of God: Creator, Redeemer, and Comforter be upon you and remain with you always. **Amen.**

Committal for a Child

At the place of interment the minister may read one or more of the following or other suitable Scripture passages:
It is not the will of God that one of these little ones should be lost. Matthew 18:14

Jesus said, "Let the little children come to me; for it is to such as these that the kingdom of God belongs."
Mark 10:14

Jesus said, "Peace I leave with you; my peace I give to you. I do not give to you as the world gives. Do not let your hearts be troubled, and do not let them be afraid."
John 14:27

Our Savior, Christ Jesus, abolished death and brought life and immortality to light through the gospel. 2 Timothy 1:10

Then shall the minister say the words of committal:
Eternal God, whose loving care is over all, we commit the earthly remains of *(Name)* to the *earth/sea/elements*, believing that *his/her* spirit is with you, whom to know is life eternal. **Amen.**

Then may be said:
The redeemed are before the throne of God, and worship God day and night within the temple, and the one who is seated on the throne will shelter them. They will hunger no more; the sun will not strike them, nor any scorching heat; for the Lamb at the center of the throne will be their shepherd and will guide them to springs of the water of life, and God will wipe away every tear from their eyes.
Revelation 7:15-17

The minister then says:
Let us pray.
God of love and grace, we entrust to your tender care this child, and to you we commit ourselves. Be our guide and comfort and give us a sure sense of your never-failing love, that in that same love and in loving memory of this child we may give ourselves to the ministry and care of children, even as Jesus, who took the little ones in his arms and blessed them. **Amen.**

God bless you and keep you. God's face shine upon you and be gracious to you. God look upon you with favor and give you peace. **Amen.**

Licensing of a Minister

This service is a recognition of those preparing for the pastoral ministry. Generally, it will take place in the student's home church as he or she begins professional training, but it may be adapted for use by a church to which the student has been called as a minister, or for a lay minister.

The licensing should be set within a full worship service and the act of licensing should take place as part of the offertory. At that time the candidate, escorted by the moderator or some other church officer, offers him or herself to be licensed to serve as a minister.

The worship leader presents an offertory prayer, saying:
We offer to you, O God, this bread and wine to be set apart for the remembrance of the self-giving of Jesus Christ; we present to you these gifts in thankfulness for your mercies to us; and we bring before you this one who is offering *himself/herself* for special ministry in your church. We also

offer ourselves, that our lives may be faithfully spent in the several ministries to which you have called us. **Amen.**

The minister then says:
The church is composed of many members with a variety of gifts, and every member is called to exercise his or her special gift in ministry. Yet the church recognizes that there are those who are called by God into church vocations for which special training is needed. It is customary for a congregation to offer a member who has made such a vocational decision a License to Minister *(or License to Preach)*. *(Name)* has offered *himself/herself* for the Christian ministry and now comes before this congregation to be confirmed in this decision by receiving a License to Minister.

The church officer escorts the candidate to a place before the table and says:
Upon recommendation of the official board and by vote of the congregation I present to *(Name)* this License to Minister. This license represents not only our endorsement of you to continue your preparation for ministry through theological study, but also our declaration of confidence in you and our way of assuring you that in your vocational preparation you have our continuing blessing and prayers.

The church officer then presents the certificate to the candidate, after which the minister asks the candidate:
(Name), do you in accepting this License to Minister promise faithfully to serve God and the church both in your study and ministry?

The candidate replies:
   I do, trusting in God's grace for help.

The minister then says to the congregation:

Do you, the members of this congregation, acknowledge and receive *(Name)* as a fully licensed minister of the gospel and promise to give *him/her* your encouragement and cooperation in the fulfillment of *his/her* calling? If so, please signify your assent by standing and uniting with me in the prayer of consecration.

Spirit of the Living God, fall afresh on *(Name)*. Consecrate *him/her* for the work of ministry. Give *him/her* wisdom to discern the mind of Christ, compassion for human need, and love toward all those to whom *he/she* is called to minister. Strengthen and nourish *his/her* faith. Make *his/her* study meaningful and *his/her* work in your church fruitful. May God's Spirit be *his/hers* this day and throughout the whole of *his/her* life. Amen.

After the prayer the newly licensed minister may be escorted to the table, where he or she shares in the administration of the Supper.

Ordination of a Minister

Ordination in the free churches is primarily for ministry in a local congregation. Thus the service of ordination is an act of a local congregation in which churches of the same denomination are invited to participate. When a church desires to present a candidate for ordination it sends out a call to nearby churches asking that a council be called to examine the candidate's qualifications for ordination to the Christian ministry. In some areas a permanent council has been established to which the call goes. The council reviews the candidate's education, hears his or her statement of Christian commitment and call to the ministry, and examines his or her doctrinal views. If the candidate proves satisfactory, the council recommends to the congregation that it proceed with the ordination.

The service of ordination is generally held at a time when representatives of the area churches and denominational leaders can attend and participate in the service. It is set in a full service of worship that generally includes the Lord's Supper. The act of ordination takes place as part of the offertory. At that time the ordinand offers him or herself to be set apart for the gospel ministry. The service given below follows the order of *The Service for the Lord's Day*, and is intended as a guide. Substitutions may be made by the presiding minister and the ordinand as they plan the order of worship.

The Service of Ordination

Affirmation of Purpose and Entry of Scriptures

> *The presiding minister begins the service with an affirmation of purpose, saying:*
> As servants of Jesus Christ we are all called to be ministers, but in addition to this general calling some are called to the church's special ministries. We are gathered today to acknowledge the call of *(Name)* to the pastoral *(if other than pastoral substitute the appropriate term, such as educational)* ministry of the church, and on behalf of the whole people of God to set *him/her* apart for this ministry through prayer and the laying on of hands. We invite all who are gathered here to join in this celebration.
>
> *As a prelude is played a layperson brings the Bible to the table, lectern, or pulpit.*

Adoration

The presiding minister or lay worship leader shall say one of the following or another suitable word of adoration, or the choir may sing an introit:

Our help is in the name of God, who made heaven and earth.
Psalm 124:8

How beautiful upon the mountains are the feet of the messenger who announces peace, who brings good news, who announces salvation, who says to Zion: "Your God reigns."
Isaiah 52:7

Rekindle the gift of God that is within you through the laying on of hands; for God did not give us a spirit of cowardice, but rather a spirit of power and of love and of self-discipline.
2 Timothy 1:6,7

Then shall be sung a hymn of praise, followed by a prayer of adoration or invocation. The presiding minister shall say:

Let us pray.

Worthy are you, O God, to receive glory, honor, and power. We praise you for the church, the body of Christ and a dwelling of your Holy Spirit. We praise you that through that same Spirit you have called men and women into your service and given them gifts fitting for such service. Especially we praise you for *(Name)*, whom we are to set apart as a minister of the gospel. Grant that this may be for *him/her* and for us a special time of joy, and may your grace be with *him/her* this day and through all the years of *his/her* ministry. **Amen.**

Confession

The presiding minister says:
If we say that we have no sin, we deceive ourselves, and the truth is not in us.   1 John 1:8

Let us therefore humbly confess our sin to God and seek forgiveness through Jesus Christ our Savior.

Then shall be offered a prayer of confession:
We confess that too often we have put stumbling blocks in the paths of our ministers. We have held back when we should have stood beside them. Forgive us. Give us grace to sustain them with prayer and enable us to support them that their service may be filled with joy and their ministries yield much fruit. These mercies we ask through Jesus Christ, who is the servant of all. Amen.

After the prayer there shall be silence in which there is personal confession of sin. The presiding minister shall then offer words of assurance:
If we confess our sins, God who is faithful and just will forgive us our sins and cleanse us from all unrighteousness.   1 John 1:9

The Gloria Patri *or a hymn of praise may be sung, after which the minister says:*

The Peace

The peace of Christ be with you.
And also with you.

The congregation and worship leaders greet one another with a handshake or an embrace and repeat the words of peace.

Ministry of the Word

The Scripture lesson(s) are read, followed by a sermon appropriate to ordination. Some suitable passages are: Exodus 3:1-14. Deuteronomy 31:14,15,23,34:9. Numbers 11:16,24-30. Isaiah 6:1-8. Jeremiah 1:4-10. Matthew 4:18-22; 28:16-20. Romans 10:13-17; 12. 1 Corinthians 12. 1 Corinthians 13. 2 Corinthians 4. Ephesians 3:7-12; 4:1-16. 1 Timothy 1:1-14; 6:12-16. 2 Timothy 1:1-1; 2:1-13; 4:1-8. 1 Peter 5:1-11.

After the sermon, the people may stand and affirm their faith by saying together a confession of faith or the church's covenant, followed by the singing of a hymn of commitment. After the hymn, prayers of petition and intercession are offered, especially praying for the ministry of the whole church.

Ministry of the Table and the Act of Ordination

The presiding minister may at this time welcome and present the other participants in the service, after which he or she says an offertory sentence. In response, the gifts are gathered and brought to the table along with the bread and wine as the Doxology is sung. At this time the candidate for ordination comes forward, escorted by the moderator of the church, as an act of offering him or herself to the special ministry of the church.

After receiving the gifts, the bread and the wine and the candidate, the presiding minister says:
Let us pray.
Gracious God, we offer to you these gifts, blessing you for the strength and skill to do our daily work. We offer to you this bread and wine to be set apart for the remembrance of

the passion of our Lord Jesus Christ. We present to you *(Name)*, who is offering *himself/herself* for the life and work of the Christian ministry, and we offer ourselves, asking you to strengthen us in your service, that we may be a living sacrifice, holy and acceptable to you this day and always. **Amen.**

The moderator presents the ordinand to the congregation, saying:

Upon recommendation of the Ordination Council of the *(Name of Area or Church)*, I have the joy of presenting *(Name)* to this congregation for ordination to the gospel ministry.

The ordinand stands and the presiding minister says to him or her:

Before God and this congregation you are called upon to answer in all truthfulness the questions I now ask you. Do you believe that you are truly called to be an ordained minister in the church of Jesus Christ and with the help of God to serve faithfully in the fulfillment of the responsibilities of this ministry?

I do, God being my helper.

Do you promise to be faithful in prayer and in the reading of the Scriptures and through study to deepen your knowledge of divine truth and human experience?

I do, God being my helper.

Will you seek to bring others into an acceptance of the cost and joy of discipleship, and through faithful teaching lead them into a full understanding of Christian commitment?

I will, God being my helper.

Will you have a loving concern for all people and give yourself to minister impartially to them without regard to race, creed, gender, or lifestyle?

I will, God being my helper.

Will you endeavor to uphold the integrity of the church and to seek that unity in which all churches will manifest the one Lord, one faith, and one baptism?

I will, God being my helper.

Will you give yourself to the denomination in which you are being ordained and in so far as possible serve its causes and seek to enlarge its witness at home and abroad?

I will, God being my helper.

The presiding minister then says:
People of God, you have heard the commitment made by *(Name)*. What is your desire?

He/She is worthy! In the name of Christ and relying on God's grace, let us ordain him/her.

Will you give *him/her* your full support in this ministry?

Relying on God's grace, we will.

Then let us acknowledge and confirm this ordination by the laying on of hands in prayer.

The presiding minister invites the ordinand to kneel and requests that those who are to share in the laying on of hands come forward and place their hands upon his or her head.

The minister then says:
From the earliest times the church has through the symbolic act of the laying on of hands and prayer recognized God's call to ministry, and by this act set apart men and women for the special ministries of the church.

Let us pray.
Eternal God, you have called *(Name)* into the special ministry of your church. Confirm that call by your Holy Spirit, as with prayer and the laying on of hands we ordain *him/*

her to the office and work of that same ministry. Grant *him/her* wisdom to understand and power to proclaim the Good News and to lead your people in worthy worship. Give *him/her* the grace to be a pastor whose love is like your own, a teacher whose store of truth brings light and understanding, and a priest who reveals your presence to every brother or sister in need. Keep *him/her* faithful to your high calling that in your good time *he/she* may hear your words, "Well done, good and faithful servant." To this ministry we consecrate *(Name)* and ourselves, that to you may be given the praise and glory, now and forever. **Amen.**

The newly ordained minister stands and the presiding minister says:

By the authority of this church and its sister churches and in the name of our Lord Jesus Christ, we declare you to be ordained to the office and work of the Christian ministry. Through this act you have been commissioned to preach and teach the Word of God, to lead the worship of the church and administer the sacraments *(ordinances)* of baptism and the Lord's Supper, to perform those other services associated with the ministry, to be a faithful pastor of your people, to inform the conscience of the congregation concerning the personal and social issues of the day, and to be a witness to those who have not come to know for themselves the love of God in Christ. I charge you in the presence of God and this company to be faithful in the commission you have received and to give yourself fully and without reservation to this ministry.

God bless you and keep you.
God's face shine upon you and be gracious to you.
God look upon you with favor and give you peace. **Amen.**

The Gloria Patri, *the Doxology, or a hymn of celebration may be sung.*

A representative of the congregation may give a Bible to the newly ordained minister, saying:
We give you this Bible of which you are commissioned as an interpreter. Make it the foundation of your life and work. Remember that "All scripture is inspired by God and is useful for teaching, for reproof, for correction, and for training in righteousness, so that everyone who belongs to God may be proficient, equipped for every good work."

2 Timothy 3:16-17

The moderator or another church official then presents the newly ordained minister with a certificate of ordination, saying:
May this certificate be a continual reminder to you that on this day and in this place you were set apart for the high and holy office of the Christian ministry.

The presiding minister leads the newly ordained minister to the table and, taking his or her right hand, says:
I welcome you into the ministry of the church of Jesus Christ. May you find joy in your ministry. On behalf of this congregation I invite you to begin this ministry as you preside in the observance of the Lord's Supper.

After the singing of a hymn the newly ordained minister takes his or her place at the table and leads the congrega-tion in the observance of the Lord's Supper as found in The Service for the Lord's Day. *If the Supper is not observed, the newly ordained minister will give the benediction. As the Bible is returned to its place by the entry the presiding minister leads the newly ordained minister to the entry way, where he or she may be greeted by the members of the congregation.*

Installation of a Minister

The service of installation may be set within *The Service for the Lord's Day*. The act of installation will then come at the time of the offertory. While the service is intended primarily for the installation of a pastor, it can be readily adapted for the installation of one of the other specialized ministers of the church, such as associate pastor, minister of Christian education, and others.

The congregation may invite a representative of the denomination or a neighboring minister to preside.

The service may be followed by a reception, at which time words of welcome may be given by church and civic representatives and a response may be made by the newly installed minister.

> *After the offerings have been dedicated, the presiding minister says:*
> Let us continue our act of dedication, as in the name of our Lord Jesus Christ, the head of the church, we install *(Name)* as pastor of this congregation.
> We shall first hear the steps that led to the call of *(Name)* to be pastor of this people. Then both pastor-elect and people shall declare their mutual covenant to one another and to God that they will endeavor to be faithful to their divine appointment and in all things seek the welfare of this church as well as the whole people of God.

A representative of the congregation then makes a statement concerning the church's selection and call of the pastor-elect.

As a hymn is sung a representative group of congregational members escorts the pastor-elect to the table, where he or she is met by the presiding minister, who says:

We believe that the call to the pastorate comes from both God and God's people. You, *(Name)*, present yourself in this place and at this time to be installed as pastor of *(Name of Church)*. Will you in all truth affirm your covenant to God and to this people?

The pastor-elect answers:

I will.

Do you affirm your faith in God, the Creator, and in Jesus Christ, the Redeemer, and in the Holy Spirit, the Abiding Presence? Do you believe that in Jesus Christ humankind has been set free from the bondage of sin and death, and that the church has been called to proclaim to the world this good news?

I do.

Do you believe that you have been truly called of God to be the pastor of this congregation?

I do.

Do you promise before God and this congregation to be a faithful teacher and preacher of the Word of God as found in the Holy Scriptures, to lead this congregation in worship that is worthy of the glory of God, to be a faithful pastor to this people and to equip them for their ministry in the world?

I will endeavor to do so, God being my helper.

The presiding minister then says to the congregation:
Do you the members of this congregation receive *(Name)* as your pastor, and before God and in the presence of one another promise to give *him/her* your loyalty and support? If so, please stand for the prayer of installation.

Prayer is then offered extempore, or as follows:
We thank you, Gracious God, for *(Name)*, who has answered the call of your people to be their pastor. Fill *him/her* with your Spirit, that *he/she* may be ready to do every good work and give a full measure of devotion as *he/she* serves in this place. Make *him/her* a faithful servant of your Word, that through *his/her* preaching and teaching those who hear may be drawn to Christ, be strengthened in their faith, and equipped for Christ's service in the world. May *he/she* be so filled with your love that *he/she* will care for all your people in their joy and sorrow, their sickness and health, their doubt and faith, standing beside them so that they may come to know the meaning of your love through *his/her* ministry. And give this congregation openness to receive this ministry for its strengthening and renewal. We pray these mercies through Jesus Christ. **Amen.**

The presiding minister then says:
In the name of Jesus Christ, I declare you, *(Name)*, to be the duly installed pastor of *(Name of Church)*.

God bless you and keep you.
God's face shine upon you and be gracious to you.
God look upon you with favor and give you peace. **Amen.**

The presiding minister, the church officers, and any others appointed to do so extend on behalf of the congregation the

Right Hand of Fellowship and welcome, as the presiding minister says:
In the name of Jesus Christ, we welcome you as pastor of *(Name of Church)*. May God's richest blessings be with you in this ministry.

The presiding minister escorts the newly installed pastor to the table to lead in the Lord's Supper and bring the service to its conclusion.

Commissioning (Ordination) of Deacons

Since earliest times deacons have occupied a special place in the church's ministry. It is therefore fitting that they should be set apart (commissioned or ordained) in a special service of the church. The commissioning or ordination of deacons should take place in *The Service for the Lord's Day* at the time of the offertory.

As the gifts are brought forward the deacons-elect, as an act of self-offering, come and take their places before the table. After the dedication of the gifts the minister addresses the congregation, saying:
Fellow members of this congregation, in the name and for the service of our Lord Jesus Christ, we are now to commission (ordain) these whom we have selected to serve in the office of deacon.

The minister or moderator then reads the names of those who are to be commissioned (ordained) and says:
These have been called to be servants of Christ and as deacons to join with the minister in the pastoral work, spiritual development, and administration of the congregation.

One or more of the following Scriptures or some other suitable passage may be read: Mark 10:42-45. Luke 22:25-27. Acts 6:1-6. Romans 12:1-13. 1 Corinthians 12:4-13.

The minister shall say to each deacon-elect:
(Name), you have been called by God through this congregation to the office of deacon. Do you promise, as God is your helper, to serve God and this congregation with all faithfulness?
 I do.

The deacons-elect then kneel. The minister and the already commissioned deacons lay their hands on them, and the minister prays extempore, or as follows:
To you, O God, we offer these chosen to serve as deacons. By your Holy Spirit give them that grace whereby they shall fulfill with devotion the duties and opportunities of their calling. Grant them wisdom rightly to administer the affairs of the congregation. May they be open to all human need, especially the needs of the hungry and the homeless, the sick and the sorrowing, the fearful and the lonely, and those who find life's burdens too heavy to bear. To this service and in the name of the one who came not to be served but to serve, we set them apart as your servants and the servants of the household of faith. **Amen.**

The newly commissioned (ordained) deacons stand and are given the Right Hand of Fellowship by the minister and their fellow deacons, after which the minister says:
May God bless you and keep you. May God's face shine upon you. May God look upon you with favor and give you peace. **Amen.**

If the Lord's Supper is to be observed, the new deacons take their places at the table to serve the Supper.

Dedication of Church Officers

The act of dedication should take place in *The Service for the Lord's Day* at the time of the offertory.

As the gifts of the people are presented, the new officers come forward and stand before the table for the act of dedication.

The minister says:
We are gathered to dedicate these who have been chosen for special service in this congregation. As they give themselves to the work of their offices, so we give ourselves to their support and encouragement and pray that they may be able to discharge their callings with faithfulness and to the glory of God.

The minister presents each of those who are to be dedicated and names the office in which they are to serve.

The minister then may read one of the following Scripture passages:
As God's chosen ones, clothe yourselves with compassion, kindness, humility, meekness, and patience. Above all, clothe yourselves with love, which binds everything together in perfect harmony. Let the peace of Christ rule in your hearts, and be thankful. Let the word of Christ dwell in you richly; teach and admonish one another in all wisdom; and with gratitude in your hearts sing psalms, hymns, and spiritual songs to God. And whatever you do, in word or deed, do everything in the name of the Lord Jesus, giving thanks to God through him.   Colossians 3:12,14-17

Do your best to present yourself to God as one approved by God, a worker who has no need to be ashamed, rightly explaining the word of truth.   2 Timothy 2:15

Like good stewards of the manifold grace of God, serve one another with whatever gift each of you has received. Whoever speaks must do so as one speaking the very words of God; whoever serves must do so with the strength that God supplies, so that God may be glorified in all things through Jesus Christ. To him belong the glory and the power forever and ever.   1 Peter 4:10-11

The minister addresses those being dedicated with these words:
You have been called to special service in this congregation. Are you willing to undertake this ministry for the glory of God? If so, will each of you answer, I am.
  I am.

Do you promise to give yourselves diligently and faithfully to this ministry? If so, answer: With God's help, I do.
  With God's help, I do.

The minister addresses the congregation, saying:
You have heard the promises of these who have been called to special service in this congregation. Let us stand and affirm our commitment to support them in their ministry.
  We are thankful that you have responded to our call and the call of God to serve in the life and work of this congregation. We promise to honor and support you in your ministry that this church may be ever faithful to its calling in Christ.

The congregation remains standing and joins in the prayer of dedication:
  Eternal God, we thank you that from among us you have chosen these persons to serve you in the ministry of this congregation. Send your Holy Spirit on

them, that they may be faithful in their service. By that same Spirit give to us the grace to support them in their tasks, that the ministry and mission of the church may go forward to your glory. Amen.

The minister may then, on behalf of the congregation, extend a welcome to the newly dedicated. As a hymn is sung they take their place among the worshipers.

Dedication of Church School Teachers and Officers

This service may be held during *The Service for the Lord's Day.*

At the time of the offertory the newly appointed church school teachers and officers come to the table and face the minister, who says:
Hear these words of Scripture:
God gives wisdom and from God's mouth come knowledge and understanding; God stores up sound wisdom for the upright and is a shield to those who walk blamelessly. Trust in God with your whole heart, and do not rely on you own insight. In all your ways acknowledge God, and your paths will be made straight. Proverbs 2:6-7; 3:5-6

Do your best to win full approval in God's sight, as a worker who is not ashamed, one who correctly teaches the message of God's truth. 2 Timothy 2:15 (GNB)

The minister, after presenting each of the appointed teachers and officers, addresses them, saying:
You have answered the call of God and of this congregation to become teachers and officers in the church school.

Do you promise to give yourself fully to this calling? If so, answer, I do.

I do.

Let us pray.

For the call that has come to these to serve as teachers and officers in the church school, we give you thanks, O God. Give them minds open to your truth and understanding hearts that they be sensitive to the needs of those whom they are called to teach and lead. Grant that they may listen with care to the questions which are asked and endeavor to answer with patience and love. May their words and their lives commend Christ to those whom they serve. Enable them to work happily as partners with their fellow teachers and officers, and do all things to your honor and glory. **Amen.**

As a hymn of commitment is sung the newly dedicated officers and teachers take their places in the congregation.

Dedication of a Church Building

The service of dedication may be in two parts: the opening of the doors and the act of dedication. Or the act of dedication may be included as part of *The Service for the Lord's Day* at the time of the offertory.

Opening of the Doors

The congregation may form a procession marching from the former church building, if nearby, or assemble before the locked doors of the new building. The minister, standing before the doors, shall say:

Lift up your heads, O gates! and be lifted up, O ancient doors! that the King of Glory may come in. Who is this King of Glory? The Lord of hosts is the King of Glory.

Psalm 24:9-10

The builder presents the keys to a representative of the congregation, who shall unlock and throw open the doors and say:
In honor of God I open the doors of this church building for the use of this congregation and as a house of prayer for all people.

Then the minister shall pray extempore or as follows:
Eternal God, as we open the doors of this house of worship and service, we open our hearts to you. Go with us as we cross this threshold, that this house may be always filled with your presence. May these doors ever be open to all persons regardless of race, color, creed, or station in life. May they be wide enough to welcome all who need your comfort and care. And may they also be the way through which your people go into the world to minister in your name. **Amen.**

Then a Doxology or a hymn may be sung as the people enter the church building.

Act of Dedication

After the people have been seated, the minister says:
Our help is in the name of God, who made heaven and earth. Unless God builds the house, those who build it labor in vain.   Psalm 124:8; 127:1

After a hymn of praise is sung the minister says:
Let us pray.

With great joy we come before you, O God. We praise you for your marvelous works among your people, but especially we praise you for this new place of worship and service brought into being by the vision and work of your people. Forgive us for any narrowness of pride that looks only upon our achievement. Give us that spirit wherein we shall with full willingness of mind and heart dedicate this building to your glory and to the service of all people. **Amen.**

The Scripture lessons shall now be read. Several suitable passages are: 1 Kings 8:12-30, 41-43. Ezra 3:10-13. Psalm 24, 84, 121. Matthew 21:1-17. Ephesians 2:13-22. 1 Peter 2:4-10. Revelation 21:15-27.

After the readings have been completed a sermon is preached, followed by the offertory. As a fitting part of the offertory the congregation presents its new building to God as a gift of thanksgiving dedicated to God's glory and service. The act of dedication may be symbolized by the laying of the blueprints or some other suitable symbol upon the table, after which the minister says:

As a congregation we are gathered about this table to dedicate this house to the glory of God and to the service of all peoples. Let us now join in the act of dedication.

To the glory of God, the Creator, Maker of heaven and earth;

To the glory of Christ, the Savior of the world;

To the glory of the Holy Spirit, the divine presence in the world:

> **We dedicate this house.**

For the worship of God;

For the reading and proclamation of God's Word;

For the celebration of the sacraments (*ordinances*) of the gospel:

We dedicate this house.

For the celebration of marriage and the strengthening of family life;

For the dedication, teaching, and guidance of children;

For the strengthening of all believers and their training as Christ's ministers in the world;

For services of memorial and bringing comfort to those who mourn;

For the work of evangelism in this community and throughout the world:

We dedicate this house.

To the memory of all whose life and love have in times past been given to the furtherance of the life and work of this congregation:

We dedicate this house.

Let us pray.

Eternal God, be present with us as we dedicate this house to your honor and glory. Grant that the worship offered in this place may be worthy of your great love and that the words of our mouths and the meditations of our hearts will be acceptable to you, our strength and our redeemer. Grant that all who come to this place, whether it be in joy or sorrow, life or death, victory or defeat, doubt or faith, sin or salvation, may find here your grace faithfully ministered. To that ministry we dedicate this house and we dedicate ourselves. **Amen.**

The congregation shall stand and say:

**We now declare this house to be set apart and conse-
crated to the worship and service of God, to whom be
glory and majesty, dominion and power, now and
forever. Amen.**

*The Lord's Supper may be celebrated, after which shall be
sung the* Gloria Patri *or a hymn of celebration. The minister then says:*

Go forth from this place into the world, there to minister
in the name of Jesus Christ. Return to this place to receive
food for life and to give glory to God.

The grace of our Lord Jesus Christ, the love of God, and
the abiding presence of the Holy Spirit go with you.
Amen.

Part 6

Worship in the Pastoral Ministry

The church's worship extends beyond the Sunday services. Through the pastor, deacons, and others, the church reaches out to homes, hospitals, and other places where members of the congregation share their joys and concerns. Whether it be a birth, illness, bereavement, or the dedication of a new home, the church should stand beside its members to enter into their joy or pain.

Materials in this section are intended to provide a pattern for worship for those occasions. They do not seek in any way to limit the freedom of the Spirit or the exercise of free worship. Rather, they point to those areas of ministry in which worship can be especially meaningful, and they provide guidelines and materials for whose involved in the exercise of such ministries.

Dedication of a Home

This service can be a part of a house-warming party in which members of the congregation and others gather with the family to celebrate their new home.

As the service begins the minister says:
We are gathered here to share with this family the joy they have in their new home, and with them to dedicate it to God, that it may become an instrument of God's love in the world. Peace be to this house, and to all who dwell in it.

Unless God builds the house, those who build it labor in vain. Psalm 127:1

How very good and pleasant it is when kindred live together in unity. Psalm 133:1

A hymn or a solo may be sung, such as "Bless This House."

The minister may then read one or more of the following passages of Scripture, or selections of his or her own choosing: Deuteronomy 6:1-7. Psalm 128. Matthew 3:3-14; 7:24-27. Luke 2:41-52; 19:1-9. John 2:1-12. Ephesians 3:14-21. Philippians 4:4-8. Colossians 3:12-21.

The Scripture reading may be followed by a brief address, after which the minister says:
Let us ask God's blessing upon this home.
O God, may your blessing come to this house and household. Grant that Jesus Christ may ever be present among those who dwell within its walls. Make this home a place with an open door and a warm hearth, ever bidding welcome to all who need hospitality and the loving embrace of a friend. Give to each member of this family a sense of being linked to every other member of our congregation and to you, O God, and to your people everywhere, that

this home may be a sign of the unity you have given to all persons in Jesus Christ, who has taught us to say when we pray:

Our Father . . .

May the peace of God rest upon this home and all who are gathered here. **Amen.**

Thanksgiving for the Birth of a Child

This service is intended primarily for the parents of the child, but may be used with the larger family.

The minister says in his or her words or the following:
As we offer thanks to God for the birth of *(Name)* and welcome *him/her* into this family, let us hear these words of Scripture.

A Scripture lesson may be read from one of the following or another suitable passage: Deuteronomy 6:4-7. Psalm 103:17-18; 127:1,3. Matthew 18:1-5. Mark 8:36-37; 10:13-16. Luke 9:46-48; 18:15-17. Colossians 3:20-21. Ephesians 6:1-4.

Prayer shall then be offered extempore, or as follows:
Creator God, open our lips, and our mouths will declare your praise.   Psalm 51:15

Let us pray.
For the universe which you have created and uphold, for its vastness and wonders:

We thank you, O God.

For your new creation in this little child:

We thank you, O God.

For the safety of *his/her* birth and the promise of a life of health and strength:

We thank you, O God.

For the skill of doctors and nurses:

We thank you, O God.

For the circle of family and friends who join with these parents in the joy which this new life has brought:

We thank you, O God.

Grant your blessing upon *(Name)* and upon *his/her* family, that *his/her* coming may deepen the bonds of love that brought *him/her* into the world. May that love sustain and nurture *him/her* and bring *him/her* into the fullness of maturity. These mercies we ask in the name of Jesus, who said, "Let the children come to me," and who taught us to say when we pray:

Our Father . . .

God bless you and keep you. God's face shine upon you and be gracious to you. God look upon you with love and give you peace.   Numbers 6:24-26

A Service for Healing

The healing of the body, mind, and spirit is an act of the God who is both Creator and Redeemer. It can be sought only in the Spirit of Christ, who prayed, "Not my will but yours be done." The service for healing should be used only after the congregation has been fully prepared.

As part of *The Service for the Lord's Day* the act of healing can come at the time of the petitions and intercessions, or it can be a special service focusing on healing. It may also take place in a home or a hospital with representatives of the congregation present, along with the minister.

The service begins as the minister reads from the following or other suitable Scripture passages: 2 Kings 4:8-37. Psalm 23; 91; 103; 145:13b-18. Matthew 4:23; 8:1-4; 8:5-13; 8:14-17; 9:2-8. Mark 6:7-13; 10:46-52; Luke 17:11-19. John 9:1-12. Acts 3:1-10; 16:16-18. Hebrews 12:1-2. James 5:13-16. 1 John 5:13-15.

The minister may then interpret the passages read and present some words concerning health and healing. If the service is included in a worship service, the minister invites any who desire healing to come forward and kneel or stand beside the minister, indicating the need for which prayer is desired. The minister then prays extempore for that person's special need, or as follows:

We praise you, Merciful God, for the loving care that you have given to *(Name)*. We now come before you with *his/her* special need. If it be in accord with your will, may *he/she* be restored to fullness of health. This mercy we pray in the name of Jesus Christ who brought healing and wholeness to those who came to him with outstretched arms and open hearts. **Amen.**

If it is the custom of the congregation, the minister may anoint with oil the person requesting healing. After the anointing the minister shall lay his or her hands upon the sick person's head and say:

Let us pray.

Eternal God, who sent Jesus Christ into the world to bring health and liberty to all, by that same power wherein he healed the sick, minister now to *(Name)*. Grant that *he/she* may be delivered from sickness and be brought to health. Give *him/her* grace to receive whatever is given to *him/her*, knowing that with you all things work together for good to those who love you. **Amen.**

After a time of silence the minister says:
May the God of peace be with you. And may your spirit, mind, and body be made whole in the presence of Jesus Christ. **Amen.**

An Order for the Taking of the Lord's Supper to Those at Home or in a Hospital

After the regular observance of the Lord's Supper it is appropriate for the minister and/or deacons to take the bread and wine that are left and share the Supper with those of the congregation who, because of illness or infirmity, are unable to be present at the worship services of the church.

The minister or deacon begins the worship with words similar to the following:
We bring you this bread and wine that have been set apart for remembrance and thanksgiving. As we eat and drink it, let us remember with thanksgiving our Lord and Savior Jesus Christ and pray that his presence will be made real to us.

Let us pray.
Gracious God, as we eat of the broken bread and drink of the cup may Jesus Christ be made known to us. Give us through him that food and drink which is nourishment for life eternal. **Amen.**

One or more of the following Scripture selections may be read: Psalm 43:3-5; 116:12-17. Isaiah 53:3-6. Mark 14:17,22- 25. Luke 24:13-35. John 6:35,51,53-55; 20:19-23. Romans 3:21-26; 5:1-11. 1 Corinthians 1:18-25. 2 Corinthians 5:7-8,14-21. 1 Timothy 2:5-6.

The readings may be followed by conversation concerning their meaning. The minister or deacon concludes the reading with the words of the institution of the Lord's Supper:
The Lord Jesus on the night when he was betrayed took a loaf of bread, and when he had given thanks, he broke it and said, "This is my body that is for you. Do this in remembrance of me." In the same way he took the cup also, after supper, saying, "This cup is the new covenant in my blood. Do this, as often as you drink it, in remembrance of me."   1 Corinthians 11:23-25

Then the minister or deacon gives thanks extempore or with one of the prayers of remembrance and thanksgiving from Part 2.

Following the prayers, the minister or deacon hands the bread to each communicant and says:
Take this bread; eat it with thanksgiving in remembrance of Jesus Christ.

After the bread has been eaten and there has been a time of silent remembrance, the minister or deacon hands the cup to each communicant and says:
Take the cup; drink of it, for it is the sign of the new covenant in Christ Jesus. Remember him with thanks as you drink it.

After the cup has been drunk and there has been a time of silence, the minister or deacon concludes the service with the Lord's Prayer and extemporaneous prayer, or as follows:
We thank you, gracious God, for bringing us to this table. In your presence help us to remember not only our Lord Jesus Christ but also our fellow church members who have

eaten of this bread and drunk of this cup. Be gracious to them, even as you are gracious to us. Use them and us to witness to your love, and grant that your church throughout the world may be strengthened in faith and be faithful to the proclamation of your truth. **Amen.**

To God's gracious mercy and protection we commit you. And the blessing of God the Creator, Christ the Redeemer, and the Holy Spirit the Living Presence be with you this day and remain with you always. **Amen.**

Part 7

Lessons for the Christian Year

The roots of a series of festivals centering upon the main events of the life of Christ and the beginning of the church go deep into the soil of the earliest Christian centuries. By the fourth century these festivals had been drawn into a yearly cycle, and gradually the Christian year as we know it today emerged. The year begins with Advent and continues through Christmas, Epiphany, Lent, Palm Sunday, Holy Week (including Maundy Thursday and Good Friday), Easter, Ascension, Pentecost, and Trinity.

Lectionaries, or tables of lessons, were developed to provide Scripture readings not only for the great festival days, but for each Sunday and weekday as well. In the Middle Ages in the West, lectionary development took place in the Roman Church, but with the Reformation the reformed bodies developed their own tables of lessons. While there were similarities in the various lectionaries, there were also many differences.

To overcome these variants and to have a lectionary that could be used ecumenically, representatives of the Roman Catholic Church and a number of Protestant churches took part in a conference in 1978 sponsored by the (North American) Consultation on Common Texts (CCT). The

Consultation developed what is known as the *Common Lectionary*. It is followed by most churches who base their worship and preaching on lectionary texts, and is the basis for the text selections in this book of worship. The *Common Lectionary* was updated in 1992; selections from that version appear on the following pages.[1]

The texts are from the Old Testament, Epistles, Gospels, and Psalms. (For a more detailed listing and further information on the lectionary, see *The Revised Common Lectionary*, by The Consultation on Common Texts, Abingdon Press, 1992.) The three-year cycle covers a sizable part of the Bible. Thus, if the lectionary is faithfully followed, a congregation, in the course of three years, will be introduced through readings and preaching to a large portion of the Scripture material.

---

[1]The *Revised Common Lectionary,* copyright 1992 by the Consultation on Common Texts.

A Suggested Lectionary for the Church Year in a Three-Year Cycle

Year A

(Begins on the First Sunday of Advent in 1992, 1995, 1998, 2001, 2004)

Sunday/Other. Day	Old Testament	Epistle	Gospel	Psalm
		ADVENT		
1st in Advent	Isa.2:1-5	Rom.13:11-14	Matt.24:36-44	122
2nd in Advent	Isa.11:1-10	Rom.15:4-13	Matt.3:1-12	72:1-7,18-19
3rd in Advent	Isa.35:1-10	Jam.5:7-10	Matt.11:2-11	146:5-10
4th in Advent	Isa.7:10-16	Rom.1:1-7	Matt.1:18-25	80:1-7,17-19
		CHRISTMAS		
Christmas Eve/Day	Isa.9:2-7	Titus 2:11-14	Luke 2:1-20	96
1st after Christmas	Isa.63:7-9	Heb.2:10-18	Matt.2:13-23	148
2nd after Christmas	Jer.31:7-14	Eph.1:3-14	John 1:1-18	147:12-20
		EPIPHANY		
Epiphany	Isa.60:1-6	Eph.3:1-12	Matt.2:1-12	72:1-7,10-14
1st after Epiphany	Isa.42:1-9	Acts 10:34-43	Matt.3:13-17	29
2nd after Epiphany	Isa.49:1-7	1 Cor.1:1-9	John 1:29-42	40:1-11
3rd after Epiphany	Isa.9:1-4	1 Cor.1:10-18	Matt.4:12-23	27:1,4-9
4th after Epiphany	Micah 6:1-8	1 Cor.1:18-31	Matt.5:1-12	15
5th after Epiphany	Isa.58:1-9a	1 Cor.2:1-12	Matt.5:13-20	112:1-9

Sunday/Other Day	Old Testament	Epistle	Gospel	Psalm
6th after Epiphany	Deut.30:15-20	1 Cor.3:1-9	Matt.5:21-37	119:1-8
7th after Epiphany	Lev.19:1-2,9-18	1 Cor.3:10-11,16-23	Matt.5:38-48	119:33-40
8th after Epiphany	Isa.49:8-16a	1 Cor.4:1-5	Matt.6:24-34	131
Last Sunday after Epiphany	Exod.24:12-18	2 Peter 1:16-21	Matt.17:1-9	2

Lent

Sunday/Other Day	Old Testament	Epistle	Gospel	Psalm
Ash Wednesday	Joel 2:1-2,12-17	2 Cor.5:20b-6:10	Matt.6:1-6,16-21	51:1-7
1st in Lent	Gen.2:15-17,3:1-7	Rom.5:12-19	Matt.4:1-11	32
2nd in Lent	Gen.12:1-4a	Rom.4:1-5,13-17	John 3:1-17	121
3rd in Lent	Exod.17:1-7	Rom.5:1-11	John 4:5-42	95
4th in Lent	1 Sam.16:1-13	Eph.5:8-14	John 9:1-41	23
5th in Lent	Ezek.37:1-14	Rom.8:6-11	John 11:1-45	130
Palm Sunday	Isa.50:4-9a	Phil.2:5-11	Matt.21:1-11	118:1-2,19-29
Maundy Thursday	Exod.12:1-14	1 Cor.11:23-26	John 13:1-7,31b-35	116:1-2,12-19
Good Friday	Isa.52:13–53:12	Heb.10:16-25	John 18:1–19:42	22

Easter

Sunday/Other Day	Old Testament	Epistle	Gospel	Psalm
Easter	Acts 10:34-43	Col.3:1-4	John 20:1-18	118:1-2,14-24
2nd of Easter	Acts 2:14a,22-32	1 Peter 1:3-9	John 20:19-31	16
3rd of Easter	Acts 2:14a,36-41	1 Peter 1:17-23	Luke 24:13-35	116:1-4,12-19
4th of Easter	Acts 2:42-47	1 Peter 2:19-25	John 10:1-10	23
5th of Easter	Acts 7:55-60	1 Peter 2:2-10	John 14:1-14	31:1-5,15-16
6th of Easter	Acts 17:22-31	1 Peter 3:13-22	John 14:15-21	66:8-20
Ascension	Acts 1:1-11	Eph.1:15-23	Luke 24:44-53	47
7th of Easter	Acts 1:6-14	1 Peter 4:12-14;5:6-11	John 17:1-11	68:1-10,32-35

Lessons for the Christian Year

Sunday/Other Day	Old Testament	Epistle	Gospel	Psalm
		PENTECOST/TRINITY/KINGDOMTIDE		
Pentecost	Acts 2:1-21	1 Cor.12:3b-13	John 20:19-23	104:24-34,35b
1st after Pentecost	Gen.1:1-2:4a	2 Cor.13:11-13	Matt.28:16-20	8
2nd after Pentecost	Gen.6:9-22; 7:24; 8:14-19	Rom.1:16-17;3:22b-28	Matt.7:21-29	46
3rd after Pentecost	Gen.12:1-9	Rom.4:13-25	Matt.9:9-13,18-26	33:1-12
4th after Pentecost	Gen.18:1-15	Rom.5:1-8	Matt.9:35-10:8	116:1-2,12-19
5th after Pentecost	Gen.21:8-21	Rom.6:1b-11	Matt.10:24-39	86:1-10,16-17
6th after Pentecost	Gen.22:1-14	Rom.6:12-23	Matt.10:40-42	13
7th after Pentecost	Gen.24:34-38, 42-49, 58-67	Rom.7:15-25a	Matt.11:16-19,25-30	45:10-17
8th after Pentecost	Gen.25:19-34	Rom.8:1-11	Matt.13:1-9,18-23	119:105-112
9th after Pentecost	Gen.28:10-19a	Rom.8:12-25	Matt.13:24-30,36-43	139:1-12,23-24
10th after Pentecost	Gen.29:15-28	Rom.8:26-39	Matt.13:31-33,44-52	105:1-11,45b
11th after Pentecost	Gen.32:22-31	Rom.9:1-5	Matt.14:13-21	17:1-7,15
12th after Pentecost	Gen.37:1-4,12-28	Rom.10:1-5	Matt.14:22-33	105:1-6,16-22
13th after Pentecost	Gen.45:1-15	Rom.11:1-2a,29-32	Matt.15:21-28	133
14th after Pentecost	Exod.1:8-2:10	Rom.12:1-8	Matt.16:13-20	124
15th after Pentecost	Exod.3:1-15	Rom.12:9-21	Matt.16:21-28	105:1-6,23-26
16th after Pentecost	Exod.12:1-14	Rom.13:8-14	Matt.18:15-20	149
17th after Pentecost	Exod.14:19-31	Rom.14:1-12	Matt.18:21-35	114
18th after Pentecost	Exod.16:2-15	Phil.1:21-30	Matt.20:1-16	105:1-6,37-45
19th after Pentecost	Exod.17:1-7	Phil.2:1-13	Matt.21:23-32	78:1-4,12-16
20th after Pentecost	Exod.20:1-4,7-9,12-20	Phil.3:4b-14	Matt.21:33-46	19

Sunday/Other Day	Old Testament	Epistle	Gospel	Psalm
21st after Pentecost	Exod.32:1-14	Phil.4:1-9	Matt.21:1-14	106:1-6;19-23
22nd after Pentecost	Exod.33:12-23	1 Thess.1:1-10	Matt.22:15-22	99
23rd after Pentecost	Deut.34:1-12	1 Thess.2:1-8	Matt.22:34-46	90:1-6,13-17
24th after Pentecost	Josh.3:7-17	1 Thess.2:9-13	Matt.23:1-12	107:1-7,33-37
25th after Pentecost	Josh.24:1-3a,14-25	1 Thess.4:13-18	Matt.25:1-13	78:1-7
26th after Pentecost	Judg.4:1-7	1 Thess.5:1-11	Matt.25:14-30	123
27th after Pentecost	Ezek.34:11-16,20-24	Eph.1:15-23	Matt.25:31-46	100

Year B

(Begins on the First Sunday of Advent in 1993, 1996, 1999, 2002, 2005)

Advent

1st in Advent	Isa.64:1-9	1 Cor.1:3-9	Mark 13:24-37	80:1-7,17-19
2nd in Advent	Isa.40:1-11	2 Peter 3:8-15a	Mark 1:1-8	85:1-2,8-13
3rd in Advent	Isa.61:1-4,8-11	1 Thess.5:16-24	John 1:6-8,19-28	126
4th in Advent	2 Sam.7:1-11,16	Rom.16:25-27	Luke 1:26-38	89:1-4,19-26

Christmas

Christmas Eve/Day	Isa.62:6-12	Titus 3:4-7	Luke 2:8-20	97
1st after Christmas	Isa.61:10-62:3	Gal.4:4-7	Luke 2:22-40	148
2nd after Christmas	Jer.31:7-14	Eph.1:3-14	John 1:10-18	147:12-20

Epiphany

Epiphany	Isa.60:1-6	Eph.3:1-12	Matt.2:1-12	72:1-7,10-14
1st after Epiphany	Gen.1:1-5	Acts 19:1-7	Mark.1:4-11	29

Sunday/Other Day	Old Testament	Epistle	Gospel	Psalm
2nd after Epiphany	1 Sam.3:1-10	1 Cor.6:12-20	John 1:43-51	139:1-6,13-18
3rd after Epiphany	Jonah 3:1-5,10	1 Cor.7:29-31	Mark 1:14-20	62:5-12
4th after Epiphany	Deut.18:15-20	1 Cor.8:1-13	Mark 1:21-28	111
5th after Epiphany	Isa.40:21-31	1 Cor.9:16-23	Mark 1:29-39	147:1-11,20c
6th after Epiphany	2 Kings 5:1-14	1 Cor.9:24-27	Mark 1:40-45	30
7th after Epiphany	Isa.43:18-25	2 Cor.1:18-22	Mark 2:1-12	41
8th after Epiphany	Hosea 2:14-20	2 Cor.3:1-6	Mark 2:13-22	103:1-13,22
Last Sunday after Epiphany	2 Kings 2:1-12	2 Cor.4:3-6	Mark 9:2-9	50:1-6

LENT

Sunday/Other Day	Old Testament	Epistle	Gospel	Psalm
Ash Wednesday	Joel 2:1-2,12-17	2 Cor.5:20b–6:10	Matt.6:1-6,16-21	51:1-17
1st in Lent	Gen.9:8-17	1 Peter 3:18-22	Mark 1:9-15	25:1-10
2nd in Lent	Gen.17:1-17,15-16	Rom.4:13-25	Mark 8:31-38	22:23-31
3rd in Lent	Exod.20:1-17	1 Cor.1:18-25	John 2:13-22	19
4th in Lent	Num.21:4-9	Eph.2:1-10	John 3:14-21	107:1-3,17-22
5th in Lent	Jer.31:31-34	Heb.5:5-10	John 12:20-33	51:1-12
Palm Sunday	Isa.50:4-9a	Phil.2:5-11	Mark 11:1-11	118:1-2,19-29
Maundy Thursday	Exod.12:1-4,11-14	1 Cor.11:23-26	John 13:1-17,31b-35	116:12-19
Good Friday	Isa.52:13–53:12	Heb.10:16-25	John 18:1–19:42	22

EASTER

Sunday/Other Day	Old Testament	Epistle	Gospel	Psalm
Easter	Isa. 25:6-9	1 Cor.15:1-11	Mark 16:1-8	118:1-2,14-24
2nd of Easter	Acts 4:32-35	1 John 1:1–2:2	John 20:19-31	133
3rd of Easter	Acts 3:12-19	1 John 3:1-7	Luke 24:36b-48	4
4th of Easter	Acts 4:5-12	1 John 3:16-24	John 10:11-18	23

Sunday/Other Day	Old Testament	Epistle	Gospel	Psalm
5th of Easter	Acts 8:26-40	1 John 4:7-12	John 15:1-8	22:25-31
6th of Easter	Acts 10:44-48	1 John 5:1-6	John 15:9-17	98
Ascension	Acts 1:1-11	Eph. 1:15-23	Luke 24:44-53	47
7th of Easter	Acts 1:15-17,21-26	1 John 5:9-13	John 17:6-19	1
		PENTECOST/TRINITY/KINGDOMTIDE		
Pentecost	Ezek.37:1-14	Rom.8:22-27	John 15:26-27; 16: 4b-15	104:24-34,35b
1st after Pentecost	Isa.6:1-8	Rom.8:12-17	John 3:1-17	29
2nd after Pentecost	1 Sam.3:1-10	2 Cor. 4:5-12	Mark 2:23–3:6	139:1-6,13-18
3rd after Pentecost	1 Sam.8:4-11,16-20	2 Cor.4:13–5:1	Mark 3:20-35	138
4th after Pentecost	1 Sam.15:34–16:13	2 Cor.5:6-10,14-17	Mark 4:26-34	20
5th after Pentecost	1 Sam.17:32-49	2 Cor.6:1-13	Mark 4:35-41	9:9-20
6th after Pentecost	2 Sam.1:1,17-27	2 Cor.8:7-15	Mark 5:21-43	130
7th after Pentecost	2 Sam.5:1-5,9-10	2 Cor.12:2-10	Mark 6:1-13	48
8th after Pentecost	2 Sam.6:1-5,12b-19	Eph.1:3-14	Mark 6:14-29	24
9th after Pentecost	2 Sam. 7:1-14a	Eph.2:11-22	Mark 6:30-34,53-56	89:20-37
10th after Pentecost	2 Sam.11:1-15	Eph.3:14-21	John 6:1-21	14
11th after Pentecost	2 Sam.11:26–12:13a	Eph.4:1-16	John 6:24-35	51:1-12
12th after Pentecost	2 Sam. 18: 5-9, 15,31-33	Eph.4:25–5:2	John 6:35,41-51	130
13th after Pentecost	1 Kings 2:10-12; 3:3-14	Eph.5:15-20	John 6:51-58	111
14th after Pentecost	1 Kings 8:22-30, 41-43	Eph.6:10-20	John 6:56-69	84

Sunday/Other Day	Old Testament	Epistle	Gospel	Psalm
15th after Pentecost	Song of Sol.2:8-13	James 1:17-27	Mark 7:1-8,14-15, 21-23	45:1-2,6-9
16th after Pentecost	Prov.22:1-2,8-9, 22-23	James 2:1-10,14-17	Mark 7:24-37	125
17th after Pentecost	Prov.1:20-33	James 3:1-12	Mark 8:27-38	19
18th after Pentecost	Prov.31:10-31	James 3:13-4:3,7-8a	Mark 9:30-37	1
19th after Pentecost	Esth.7:1-6, 9-10;9:20-22	James 5:13-20	Mark 9:38-50	124
20th after Pentecost	Job 1:1;2:1-10	Heb.1:1-4,2:5-12	Mark 10:2-16	26
21st after Pentecost	Job 23:1-9,16-17	Heb.4:12-16	Mark 10:17-31	22:1-15
22nd after Pentecost	Job 38:1-7	Heb.5:1-10	Mark 10:35-45	104:1-9,24,35c
23rd after Pentecost	Job 42:1-6,10-17	Heb.7:23-28	Mark 10:46-52	34:1-8
24th after Pentecost	Ruth 1:1-18	Heb.9:11-14	Mark 12:28-34	146
25th after Pentecost	Ruth 3:1-5;4:13-17	Heb.9:24-28	Mark 12:38-44	127
26th after Pentecost	1 Sam.1:4-20	Heb.10:11-14,19-25	Mark 13:1-8	16
27th after Pentecost	2 Sam.23:1-7	Rev.1:4b-8	John 18:33-37	132:1-12

Year C

ADVENT

(Begins on the First Sunday of Advent in 1994, 1997, 2000, 2003)

Sunday/Other Day	Old Testament	Epistle	Gospel	Psalm
1st in Advent	Jer.33:14-16	1 Thess.3:9-13	Luke 21:25-36	25:1-10
2nd in Advent	Malachi 3:1-4	Phil.1:3-11	Luke 3:1-6	Luke 1:68-79
3rd in Advent	Zeph.3:14-20	Phil.4:4-7	Luke 3:7-18	Isa.12:2-6
4th in Advent	Micah 5:2-5a	Heb.10:5-10	Luke 1:39-45	80:1-7

Sunday/Other Day	Old Testament	Epistle	Gospel	Psalm
		CHRISTMAS		
Christmas Eve/Day	Isa.52:7-10	Heb.1:1-4	John 1:1-14	98
1st after Christmas	1 Sam.2:18-20,26	Col.3:12-17	Luke 2:41-52	148
2nd after Christmas	Num.6:22-27	Gal.4:4-7	Luke 2:15-21	8
		EPIPHANY		
Epiphany	Isa.60:1-6	Eph.3:1-12	Matt.2:1-12	72:1-7,10-14
1st after Epiphany	Isa.43:1-7	Acts 8:14-17	Luke 3:15-17,21-22	29
2nd after Epiphany	Isa.62:1-5	1 Cor.12:1-11	John 2:1-11	36:5-10
3rd after Epiphany	Neh.8:1-3,5-6,8-10	1 Cor.12:12-31a	Luke 4:14-21	19
4th after Epiphany	Jer.1:4-10	1 Cor.13:1-13	Luke 4:21-30	71:1-6
5th after Epiphany	Isa.6:1-8	1 Cor.15:1-11	Luke 5:1-11	138
6th after Epiphany	Jer.17:5-10	1 Cor.15:12-20	Luke 6:17-26	1
7th after Epiphany	Gen.45:3-11,15	1 Cor.15:35-38,42-50	Luke 6:27-38	37:1-11,39-40
8th after Epiphany	Isa.55:10-13	1 Cor.15:51-58	Luke 6:39-49	92:1-4,12-15
Last Sunday after Epiphany	Exod.34:29-35	2 Cor.3:12-4:2	Luke 9:28-36	99
		LENT		
Ash Wednesday	Joel 2:1-2,12-17	2 Cor.5:20b-6:10	Matt.6:1-6,16-21	51:1-17
1st in Lent	Deut.26:1-11	Rom.10:8b-13	Luke 4:1-13	91:1-2,9-16
2nd in Lent	Gen.15:1-12,17-18	Phil.3:17-4:1	Luke 13:31-35	27
3rd in Lent	Isa.55:1-9	1 Cor.10:1-13	Luke 13:1-9	63:1-8
4th in Lent	Joshua 5:9-12	2 Cor.5:16-21	Luke 15:1-3,11b-32	32
5th in Lent	Isa.43:16-21	Phil.3:4b-14	John 12:1-8	126

Sunday/Other Day	Old Testament	Epistle	Gospel	Psalm
Palm Sunday	Isa.50:4-9a	Phil.2:5-11	Luke 22:14-23:56	31:9-16
Maundy Thursday	Exod.12:1-4,11-14	1 Cor.11:23-26	John 13:1-17,31b-35	116:1-2,12-19
Good Friday	Isa.52:13–53:12	Heb.10:16-25	John 18:1–19:42	22
		EASTER		
Easter	Acts 10:34-43	1 Cor.15:19-26	John 20:1-18	118:1-2,14-24
2nd of Easter	Acts 5:27-32	Rev.1:4-8	John 20:19-31	150
3rd of Easter	Acts 9:1-6	Rev.5:11-14	John 21:1-19	30
4th of Easter	Acts 9:36-43	Rev.7:9-17	John 10:22-30	23
5th of Easter	Acts 11:1-18	Rev.21:1-6	John 13:31-35	148
6th of Easter	Acts 16:9-15	Rev.21:10,22–22:5	John 14:23-29	67
Ascension	Acts 1:1-11	Eph.1:15-23	Luke 24:44-53	47
7th of Easter	Acts 16:16-34	Rev.22:12-14, 16-17, 20-21	John 17:20-26	97
		PENTECOST/TRINITY/KINGDOMTIDE		
Pentecost	Acts 2:1-21	Rom.8:14-17	John 14:8-17	104:24-34,35b
1st after Pentecost	Prov.8:1-4,22-31	Rom.5:1-5	John 16:12-15	8
2nd after Pentecost	1 Kings 8:20-21, 30-39	Gal.1:1-12	Luke 7:1-10	96
3rd after Pentecost	1 Kings 17:8-16	Gal.1:11-24	Luke 7:11-17	146
4th after Pentecost	1 Kings 21:1-10, 15-21a	Gal.2:15-21	Luke 7:36–8:3	5:1-8
5th after Pentecost	1 Kings 19:1-4, 8-15a	Gal.3:23-29	Luke 8:26-39	42 & 43
6th after Pentecost	2 Kings 2:1-2,6-14	Gal.5:1,13-25	Luke 9:51-62	77:1-2,11-20

Sunday/Other Day	Old Testament	Epistle	Gospel	Psalm
7th after Pentecost	2 Kings 5:1-14	Gal.6:7-16	Luke 10:1-11,16-20	30
8th after Pentecost	Amos 7:7-17	Col.1:1-14	Luke 10:25-37	82
9th after Pentecost	Amos 8:1-12	Col.1:15-28	Luke 10:38-42	52
10th after Pentecost	Hosea 1:2-10	Col.2:6-15	Luke 11:1-13	85
11th after Pentecost	Hosea 11:1-11	Col.3:1-11	Luke 12:13-21	107:1-9,43
12th after Pentecost	Isa.1:1,10-20	Heb.11:1-3,8-16	Luke 12:32-40	50:1-8,22-23
13th after Pentecost	Isa.5:1-7	Heb.11:29–12:2	Luke 12:49-56	80:1-2,8-19
14th after Pentecost	Jer.1:4-10	Heb.12:18-29	Luke 13:10-17	71:1-6
15th after Pentecost	Jer.2:4-13	Heb.13:1-8,15-16	Luke 14:1,7-14	81:1,10-16
16th after Pentecost	Jer.18:1-11	Philemon 1-21	Luke 14:25-33	139:1-6,13-18
17th after Pentecost	Jer.4:11-12,22-28	1 Tim.1:12-17	Luke 15:1-10	14
18th after Pentecost	Jer.8:18–9:1	1 Tim.2:1-7	Luke 16:1-13	79:1-9
19th after Pentecost	Jer.32:1-3a,6-15	1 Tim.6:6-19	Luke 16:19-31	91:1-6,14-16
20th after Pentecost	Lam.1:1-6	2 Tim.1:1-14	Luke 17:5-10	137
21st after Pentecost	Jer.29:1,4-7	2 Tim.2:8-15	Luke 17:11-19	66:1-12
22nd after Pentecost	Jer.31:27-34	2 Tim.3:14–4:5	Luke 18:1-8	119:97-104
23rd after Pentecost	Joel 2:23-32	2 Tim.4:6-8,16-18	Luke 18:9-14	65
24th after Pentecost	Hab.1:1-4;2:1-4	2 Thess.1:1-4,11-12	Luke 19:1-10	119:137-144
25th after Pentecost	Hag.1:15b-2:9	2 Thess.2:1-5,13-17	Luke 20:27-38	145:1-5,17-21
26th after Pentecost	Isa.65:17-25	2 Thess.3:6-13	Luke 21:5-19	98
27th after Pentecost	Jer.23:1-6	Col.1:11-20	Luke 23:33-43	46

Glossary

This glossary contains brief definitions of some of the more common worship terms. Fuller explanations, as well as many more items, can be found in J. G. Davies, *The New Westminster Dictionary of Liturgy and Worship* (Philadelphia: Westminster Press, 1986).

Advent (Latin *adventus*: arrival, coming) A period of preparation for the celebration of Christ's coming beginning with the fourth Sunday before Christmas.

Agnus Dei (Latin: Lamb of God) An antiphonal prayer or anthem asking for divine mercy.

Amen From the Hebrew, meaning *firm* or *established*, or, as an adverb, *certainly* or *assuredly*. Often used by Jesus at the beginning of a saying and translated *verily* or *truly*. In worship *amen* is often used as a congregational response to prayer.

Anamnesis From the Greek, meaning *to remember*. In worship it is the prayer of remembrance of Jesus Christ in the Lord's Supper.

Ascription A form of prayer giving (ascribing) glory to God, usually following the sermon or at the end of the service.

Benedictus (Latin from *benedicere*: to bless) A canticle from the Gospel of Luke (1:68-79).

Canticle (Latin *canticulum*: little song) A biblical hymn, such as the *Benedictus, Magnificat,* or *Nunc Dimittis*.

Ceremonial Formal actions, such as the kiss of peace, the breaking of the bread, or the laying on of hands, that are a part of worship, as distinct from ritual, which refers to the words of worship.

Communicant (Latin from *communicare*: to receive communion) One who receives the Lord's Supper, or one who is entitled to receive the Supper, generally a church member.

Creed (Latin *credo*: I believe) The first word of the Apostles' and Nicene Creeds; an affirmation of religious belief.

Doxology (Greek *doxologia*: literally, words of glory) An ascription of praise, usually trinitarian.

Epiclesis A Greek word denoting the prayer in the Lord's Supper and baptism for the presence of the Holy Spirit.

Epiphany (Greek *epiphaneia*: manifestation) Celebration of the coming of the wise men as the first manifestation of Christ to the Gentiles, and of the baptism of Jesus.

Eucharist A Greek term meaning gratitude or thanksgiving, used in some churches for the Lord's Supper and in others for the entire service which includes the Lord's Supper. Also used for the prayer of thanks in the Lord's Supper.

Fraction The breaking of the bread in the Lord's Supper.

Gloria in Excelsis A fourth-century Latin hymn based on the angels' song (Luke 2:14).

Gloria Patri (Latin: glory to the Father) A declaration of glory to God, usually in trinitarian form.

Intinction (Latin *intingo*: I dip in) The action in the Lord's Supper of dipping the bread into the wine so that both are consumed at the same time.

Introit (from Latin *introire*: to go in) In Protestant worship, a musical selection sung or played at the beginning the service.

Jubilate Deo A declaration of joy based on Psalm 100.

Kyrie (Greek *kyrie eleison*: Lord have mercy) The people's petition to Christ for mercy.

Lectionary A list of lessons from the Scriptures covering the Christian year.

Lent (Middle English *lente*: springtime) Measured by the forty weekdays from Ash Wednesday to Easter. Traditionally a time of self-examination and fasting.

Litany (Greek *litaneia*: entreaty, petition) A responsive prayer in which a leader offers petitions that are answered by the congregation, often with an unchanging response.

Liturgy (Greek *leitourgia*: a work or service of the people) A form for worship followed by a congregation.

Love Feast or Agape A common meal in which Christians gather to express their mutual love for one another in Christ.

Magnificat (Latin from *magnificare*: to magnify, extol) Mary's song of praise (Luke 1:46-55).

Maundy Thursday (Latin *mandatum novum*: a new commandment) Based upon the command given by Jesus in John 13:34 and associated with the Last Supper. Often a congregational meal takes place which concludes with the observance of the Lord's Supper. Some churches include footwashing.

Nunc Dimittis (Latin: now dismiss) The song of Simeon (Luke 2:29-35).

Offertory The act of worship that begins the Liturgy of the Table, consisting of the gifts of the people, their self-dedication, and the offering of the bread and the wine for the Lord's Supper.

Ordinance (Latin *ordinans* from *ordinare*: to put in order, ordain or command) Used in some churches to refer to baptism and the Lord's Supper as based upon the commands of Jesus.

Paschal or Christ Candle The candle symbolizing the risen Christ is lit on Easter Eve and remains lit until Pentecost, when it is extinguished, to be relit when baptism (symbolizing the death and resurrection of Christ) is celebrated.

Pentecost A celebration of the gift of the Holy Spirit, observed fifty days after Easter.

Rite A formal act constituting a religious observance.

Ritual The words established for a religious observance.

Rubrics (Latin from *ruber*: red) Directions for services of worship, sometimes printed in red.

Sacrament (Latin *sacramentum*: oath of allegiance, generally of a soldier to a commander) In free-church worship the term refers to baptism and the Lord's Supper.

Sanctus A threefold "Holy, holy, holy" adapted from Isaiah 6:3, said or sung before the prayer of thanksgiving in the Lord's Supper.

Sursum Corda (Latin: lift up your hearts) A versicle and response inviting the congregation to join in thanksgiving to God.

Te Deum Laudamus (Latin: You, God, we praise) An ancient hymn of praise.

Versicle (Latin *versiculus*: a short line or verse) A short sentence said by the worship leader, usually followed by a congregational response and often used to introduce a prayer.

Additional Worship Resources Published by Judson Press

A Message in a Minute: Lighthearted Minidramas for Churches, William D. Wolfe with Sheryl J. Anderson

Dedication Services for Every Occasion, Manfred Holck, Jr.

Litanies for All Occasions, Garth House

Open to Glory: Renewing Worship in the Congregation, Carol Doran, Thomas H. Troeger

Prayers: From Adoration to Zeal, C. Welton Gaddy

Prayers for All Occasions: For Pastors and Lay Leaders, Roy Pearson

Word, Water, Wine and Bread, William H. Willimon (Traces the history of worship as it reveals the story of our continuing relationship with God.)

Writing Your Own Worship Materials, G. Temp Sparkman